how to
Teach
English

An introduction to the practice of English language teaching

Jeremy Harmer

Longman

Pearson Education Limited

Edinburgh Gate, Harlow, Essex CM20 2JE. England
and Associated Companies throughout the World.

www.longman.com

First published 1998

Tenth impression 2003

Printed in Malaysia

ISBN 0582 29796 6

Acknowledgements
We are grateful to the following for permission to reproduce copyright material:
Addison Wesley Longman for an extract from the *Longman Dictionary of
Contemporary English*; Cambridge University Press for extracts from *Language in Use,
Pre-Intermediate* by A. Doff and C. Jones, *Language in Use, Intermediate*
by A. Doff and C. Jones, and *True to Life, Intermediate* by R. Gairns and
S. Redman; Heinemann Educational Books for an extract from *Reward Intermediate*
by S. Greenall; Henry Holt & Co Inc for an adapted and complete version of the
poem 'Fire and Ice' from *The Poetry of Robert Frost*, edited by Edward Connery
Lathem. Copyright 1951 by Robert Frost, copyright 1923, © 1969 by Henry Holt &
Co Inc.

Illustrated by A.M. McLoughlin and Eric Smith.

We are grateful to the following for permission to reproduce copyright photographs:
Getty Images/Frank Ore for 75tr, Greg Evans/gei/M.Wells for 75tl, Heinemann
Publishing for page 168, The Image Bank/Frank Ore for 75tr, Olivetti Computers
for 178, Panasonic for 183, Superstock for 157, Telegraph Colour Library/Masterfile
for 75bl.

Commissioned photography by: Gareth Boden Photography.

We have been unable to trace the copyright holder for the photograph on page 115
and would be grateful for any information that would enable us to do so.

For Tanya –
just in case

Contents

Acknowledgements

A number of people have influenced the development of *How to Teach English* and have changed the lonely job of writing into something much more like real collaboration – whether directly or indirectly.

I am especially grateful to Richard Rossner, as always. The *Engage–Study–Activate* description was developed with him in the first place in a book we wrote together and his reading of Chapter 4 – and comments on it – have proved extremely useful. Anita Harmer's reactions in snatches of conversation amongst the rituals of daily life have, as ever, been completely indispensable.

I was fortunate to start work on this book when Melanie Butler was in charge of the methodology list at Addison Wesley Longman. Her many suggestions, encouragements and off-the-wall commentaries (a speciality of hers) helped to tease out many of the issues implicit in a work of this nature. David Lott's guidance and his contribution to the final version of the book have been immeasurable.

Along the way, I have been incredibly lucky in the reports I have received from Gill Stacey, Sue Jones and Rodney Blakeston who between them helped to clarify parts of the book. Maggy McNorton and her students at the University of Glamorgan were vital in the development of style and content. Her students' robust feedback and trenchant comments were immensely stimulating. At a later stage, Martin Parrott's insightful reactions were absolutely invaluable, as were the comments of David Riddell and his CELTA trainees at Kingsway College, London – invigorating reactions from both sides! Terry Tomscha's help was also greatly appreciated.

To all these people I offer my profound gratitude. I only hope that they will like the way it has turned out!

Jeremy Harmer
Cambridge

Introduction

Who is the book for?   *How to Teach English* is a book designed for people at the start of their teaching career, at that stage where they are just about to do – or have just done – an initial teacher training course. It is written for people who teach mostly adults of whatever age.

What is it about?   *How to Teach English* is about teaching English as a foreign or second language: what it is about, and how to do it. Here is what it contains.

- The first two chapters discuss general issues about teaching and learning: how to be a good teacher, how to be a good learner.
- Chapter 3 looks at issues that help teachers to manage classes better – using their physical presence and voices, and organising the room and students in a variety of ways.
- Chapter 4 suggests a way of looking at all teaching and learning – a way which helps teachers to decide how to put teaching sequences together.
- Chapter 5 is about the language itself. It introduces some basic concepts of grammar, vocabulary, language use, pronunciation and punctuation and is intended for new teachers who may have little experience in this area.
- Chapter 6 looks at the various options for studying language, from very teacher-led presentations to rather more learner-centred 'discovery' activities.
- Chapters 7–10 look at examples for teaching the so-called 'four skills' (reading, writing, speaking and listening).
- Chapter 11 discusses how teachers should use textbooks – should they be followed slavishly or adapted to the teacher and the students' particular needs?
- Chapter 12 looks at why teachers need to plan their lessons and how they can do so.
- The final chapter (called 'What if?') deals with problems which teachers frequently encounter. How, if at all, can they be resolved?
- The Task File at the back of the book comprises a large number of exercises and activities designed to predict and/or build on the information in the chapters of the main book. These are intended to be photocopied for use on training courses or to be used by individual teachers working on their own.
- The book ends with three appendices. One describes equipment commonly in use in the classroom. The second gives suggestions for further reading, and the third contains the phonetic alphabet and some examples of phonetic script.

How to Teach English is a practical book, concentrating on examples of teaching and teaching practice rather than on a detailed analysis of learning theory. It aims to give a general picture – with examples showing procedures for beginners, elementary and intermediate students, and procedures reflecting a range of current teaching and learning styles.

Teachers and potential teachers may want to read *How to Teach English* from cover to cover before they start a training course. They will then have a general overview of the profession and what it entails.

During a course, however, readers may want to skip around, looking at individual chapters as and when the topics come up. However, the *Engage–Study–Activate* description in Chapter 4 is crucial, since much of the subsequent material flows from it.

Readers may also want to start by looking at the Task File for a particular chapter before actually reading the chapter. That way, they can see if their opinions and conclusions coincide with the author's. This will depend on the nature of the task.

Finally, the teacher is referred to throughout the book as 'he', 'she' and 'they' in about equal proportions. Gender and pronoun usage look set to bedevil the English language for some years yet!

How to be a good teacher

- What makes a good teacher?
- How should teachers talk to students?
- How should teachers give instructions?
- Who should talk in class?
- What are the best kinds of lesson?
- How important is it to follow a pre-arranged plan?

What makes a good teacher?

In an attempt to find out what we all think about teachers and teaching I recently asked a variety of people the question 'What makes a good teacher?' I was especially interested to see what their instant response would be since that might throw some light upon deeply-held beliefs about this fundamental part of human experience.

Many different people were asked the question, almost always with a tape machine there to record their answers. There were teachers of English in the UK, in Spain and from Finland. Some of the respondents were teacher trainers and methodologists. Last – but by no means least – I interviewed students of different nationalities studying at private language schools in Britain, and secondary school students studying at a Cambridge comprehensive school.

The following answers are representative of the many that were given.

⇨ *They should make their lessons interesting so you don't fall asleep in them.*
This was said by an adult student at a private language school in England.

⇨ *A teacher must love her job. If she really enjoys her job that'll make the lessons more interesting.*
This was also said by an adult student in England. Teachers who look fed up or unhappy with what they are doing tend to have a negative effect on their students. When you observe good teachers you will notice that, even when/if they are feeling terrible (outside the classroom), they put on a good 'teacher's face' when they enter the classroom.

⇨ *I like the teacher who has his own personality and doesn't hide it from the students so that he is not only a teacher but a person as well – and it comes through the lessons.*
Students tend to be interested in their teachers – at least at first. The

ones who share their personality with their classes often have better results than those who don't.

⇨ *I like a teacher who has lots of knowledge, not only of his subject.*
The preoccupation with the teacher's personality is reflected here too: teachers should not be afraid to bring their own interests and lives into the classroom (within reason, of course).

⇨ *A good teacher is an entertainer and I mean that in a positive sense, not a negative sense.*
Students enjoy being entertained and amused. However, a balance has to be struck between entertainment (which often gives teachers enjoyable feedback) and teaching/learning. Sometimes, the former can overwhelm the latter.

Although, as we can see, the character and personality of the teacher is a crucial issue in the classroom, by far the greatest number of responses to the question 'What makes a good teacher?' were not so much about teachers themselves, but rather about the relationship between the teacher and the students. This is borne out in the following responses.

⇨ *It's important that you can talk to the teacher when you have problems and you don't get along with the subject.*
These are the words of an adult student. Teachers must be approachable.

⇨ *A good teacher is ... somebody who has an affinity with the students that they're teaching.*
Successful teachers are those people who can identify with the hopes, aspirations and difficulties of their students while they are teaching them.

⇨ *A good teacher should try and draw out the quiet ones and control the more talkative ones.*
Experienced teachers can tell you of classes which are dominated by bright, witty, loud, extrovert students. As this EFL teacher implies, it's easy to be captivated by such students. It takes more effort to ensure that the quiet, shyer students also get a chance. One of the secondary students I questioned said, 'A good teacher is ... someone who asks the people who don't always put their hands up.'

⇨ *He should be able to correct people without offending them.*
Explaining to students that they have made a mistake is one of the most perilous encounters in the classroom. It has to be done with tact. The teacher has to measure what is appropriate for a particular student in a particular situation.

⇨ *A good teacher is ... someone who helps rather than shouts.*
Said by a secondary school student, this was one of the many comments about discipline. The people who resent bad behaviour most are not teachers, but other students who feel their time is being wasted. Learning how to manage students and how to control boisterous classes is one of the fundamental skills of teaching.

⇨ *A good teacher is ... someone who knows our names.*

Class management – the ability to control and inspire a class – is one of the fundamental skills of teaching. Teachers find it much easier if their students believe that they are genuinely interested in them and available for them.

In a book of research called *Making Sense of Teaching*, the authors Sally Brown and Donald McIntyre selected a group of good teachers, chosen by their pupils. They wanted to find out how these 'good teachers' did their job so they asked them about their teaching. This is what they found out.

> The most obvious common feature of the different *teachers' accounts* was that in response to our question about their teaching they almost always talked about what *their pupils* were doing.

A simple answer to the question 'What makes a good teacher?' therefore, is that good teachers care more about their students' learning than they do about their own teaching.

Teachers can never be quite sure what their students think of them, however. The least predictable things can affect their pupils' perception. One 13-year-old girl was adamant that 'The teacher needs to have dress sense – not always the same old boring suits and ties!'

How should teachers talk to students?

The way that teachers talk to students – the manner in which they interact with them – is one of the crucial teacher skills, but it does not demand technical expertise. It does, however, require teachers to empathise with the people they are talking to.

One group of people who seem to find it fairly natural to adapt their language to their audience are parents when they talk to their young children. Studies show that they use more exaggerated tones of voice, and speak with less complex grammatical structures than they would if they were talking to adults. Their vocabulary is generally more restricted too and the attempt to make eye contact (and other forms of physical contact) is greater. They generally do these things unconsciously.

Though teachers and students are not the same as parents and children, this subconscious ability to 'rough-tune' the language is a skill they have in common. Rough-tuning is that unconscious simplification which both parents and teachers make. Neither group sets out to get the level of language exactly correct for their audience. They rely, instead, on a general perception of what is being understood by the people listening to them. Their empathy allows them to almost feel whether the level of language they are using is appropriate for the audience they are addressing.

Experienced teachers rough-tune the way they speak to students as a matter of course. Newer teachers need to concentrate their focus on their students' comprehension as the yardstick by which to measure their own speaking style in the classroom.

Apart from adapting their language, experienced teachers also use physical movement: gestures, expressions, mime. It becomes almost second nature to show happiness and sadness, movement and time sequences, concepts (e.g. 'heavy' and 'drunk') using these techniques. They become part of the language teachers use, especially with students at lower levels.

How should teachers give instructions?

This issue of how to talk to students becomes crucial when teachers are giving their students instructions. The best activity in the world is a waste of time if the students don't understand what it is they are supposed to do.

There are two general rules for giving instructions: they must be kept as simple as possible, and they must be logical. Before giving instructions, therefore, teachers must ask themselves the following questions: What is the important information I am trying to convey? What must the students know if they are to complete this activity successfully? Which information do they need first? Which should come next?

When teachers give instructions, it is important for them to check that the students have understood what they are being asked to do. This can be achieved either by asking a student to explain the activity after the teacher has given the instruction or by getting someone to show the other people in the class how the exercise works. Where students all share the same mother tongue (which the teacher also understands), a member of the class can be asked to translate the instructions as a check that they have understood them.

Who should talk in class?

There is a continuing debate about the amount of time teachers should spend talking in class. Trainees' classes are sometimes criticised because there is too much TTT (Teacher Talking Time) and not enough STT (Student Talking Time).

As we shall see in Chapter 4, getting students to speak – to use the language they are learning – is a vital part of a teacher's job. Students are the people who need the practice, in other words, not the teacher. In general terms, therefore, a good teacher maximises STT and minimises TTT.

Good TTT may have beneficial qualities, however. If teachers know how to talk to students – if they know how to rough-tune their language to the students' level, as we have discussed above – then the students get a chance to hear language which is certainly above their own productive level, but which they can more or less understand. Such 'comprehensible input' (a term coined by the American methodologist Stephen Krashen) – where students receive rough-tuned input in a relaxed and unthreatening way – is an important feature in language acquisition. TTT works!

A classroom where the teacher's voice drones on and on day after day and where you hardly ever hear the students say anything is not one that most teachers and students would approve of, however. TTT can be terribly over-used. Conversely, a class where the teacher seems reluctant to speak is not very attractive either.

The best lessons are ones where STT is maximised, but where at appropriate moments during the lesson the teacher is not afraid to summarise what is happening, tell a story, enter into discussion etc. Good teachers use their common sense and experience to get the balance right.

What are the best kinds of lesson?

One of the greatest enemies of successful teaching is student boredom. This is often caused by the deadening predictability of much classroom time. Students frequently know what is going to happen in class and they know this because it will be the same as what happened in the last class – and a whole string of classes before that. Something has to be done to break the chain.

In his monumental book, *Breaking Rules*, John Fanselow suggests that, both for the teacher's sanity and the students' continuing involvement, teachers need to violate their own behaviour patterns. If a teacher normally teaches in casual clothes, he should turn up one day wearing a suit. If a teacher normally sits down, she should stand up. If he or she is normally noisy and energetic as a teacher, he or she should spend a class behaving calmly and slowly. Each time teachers break one of their own rules, in other words, they send a ripple through the class. That ripple is a mixture of surprise and curiosity and it is a perfect starting point for student involvement.

The need for surprise and variety within a fifty-minute lesson is also overwhelming. If, for example, students spend all of that time writing sentences, they will probably get bored. But if, in that fifty minutes, there are a number of different tasks with a selection of different topics, the students are much more likely to remain interested. This can be seen most clearly with children at primary and secondary levels, but even adults need a varied diet to keep them stimulated.

However, variety is not the same as anarchy. Despite what we have said, students tend to like a certain amount of predictability: they appreciate a safe structure which they can rely on. And too much chopping and changing – too much variety in a fifty-minute lesson – can be destabilising. Good teachers find a balance between predictable safety and unexpected variety.

How important is it to follow a pre-arranged plan?

It is one thing to be able to plan lessons which will have variety – an issue we will look at in Chapter 12 – but being *flexible* when the class is actually taking place is another matter altogether. Once again, a balance has to be struck between teachers attempting to achieve what they set out to achieve on the one hand and responding to what students are saying or doing on the other.

Suppose that the teacher has planned that the students should prepare a dialogue and then act it out, after which there is a reading text and some exercises for them to get through. The teacher has allowed twenty minutes for dialogue preparation and acting out. But when the students start working on this activity, it is obvious that they need more time. The teacher then discovers that they would like to spend at least half the lesson on just the acting-out phase which they are finding helpful and enjoyable. At that moment, he or she has to decide whether to abandon the original plan and go along with the students' wishes or whether it is better to press ahead regardless.

Another scenario is also possible: all the students are still working on a dialogue preparation except for two pairs who have already finished. The teacher then has to decide whether to tell them to wait for the others to catch up (which might make them bored and resentful) or whether to stop the rest of the class to prevent this. Then the other students might end up feeling frustrated because they didn't have a chance to finish.

There are other crises too: the tape recorder suddenly doesn't work; the teacher has forgotten to bring the material they were relying on; the students look at the planned reading text and say 'We've done that before'.

Good teachers are flexible enough to cope with these situations. Because they are focusing on the students and what they need, they are able to react quickly to the unplanned event. Perhaps, in the case of the pairs who finish early, for example, they have a couple of quick useful tasks 'up their sleeves' which they can ask the pairs to do while they're waiting. Good teachers recognise that their plans are only prototypes and they may have to abandon some or all of them if things are going too fast or too slow. Good teachers are flexible.

Conclusions

In this chapter we have
- described some of the qualities which good teachers possess: an ability to give interesting classes, using the full range of their personality; the desire to empathise with students, treating them all equally however tempting it is to do otherwise; and 'knowing all their names'.
- investigated the kind of language teachers use with students. It should at all times be comprehensible, and, especially when giving instructions, it should be clear and well staged.
- discussed the relative merits of Student Talking Time and Teacher Talking Time. TTT can have uses – helping students to acquire language – but should not predominate at the expense of STT.
- stressed the need for variety within a secure setting. We have said that teachers need to walk a fine line between predictability and surprise, without lurching into either monotony or anarchy.
- concentrated on the teacher's ability to respond flexibly to what happens in class, even while attempting to follow a pre-arranged plan.

Looking ahead

- Many of the issues about the teacher's rapport with students will come up in Chapters 6–10 when we look at teaching techniques.
- Issues of variety and flexibility are absolutely crucial to the planning of lessons. You will find that these concepts resurface in Chapter 12.
- Since we have spent this opening chapter discussing what makes a good teacher, the next chapter looks the other way and considers what makes a good learner. Are some people better at it than others? Why?

How to be a good learner

- Why is it difficult to describe a good learner?
- How important is the students' motivation?
- Who is responsible for learning?
- What characteristics do good classroom learners share?
- What's special about teaching adults?
- What are the different levels?
- How should we teach the different levels?

Why is it difficult to describe a good learner?

Many factors need to be taken into account when considering the qualities of good learners. What are their backgrounds, for example, their past learning experiences? Why are they in the classroom? Why is one study method appropriate for student A but not for Student B? Because each student brings a unique personality to the classroom, it is often difficult to assess the factors involved.

Research results don't necessarily tell us what we really want to know either. For example, a recent university research team in Britain wanted to find out why some children who learned musical instruments became very good at it while others remained at best competent. They found that the most common factor was simply the number of hours the children had practised.

It is comforting when old sayings like 'practice makes perfect' come true! But the research still leaves us with questions. It doesn't tell us why some children practise more than others, nor about the type of practice they do. Neither does it account for those exceptional children who become expert players even when they do not practise as much as others.

Teachers have some commonly-held views about good learners. Anecdotally, they will tell you that the students who do best are the ones who always do their homework, for example. We might be able to say, therefore, that doing homework is the trademark of a good learner. But again we are left with questions. Why do some people do homework while others don't? Why do some exceptional students succeed who don't do homework? Is it the homework itself that makes the difference or the underlying state of mind of the student?

What we need to find out is whether there are any generalisations which will help us to encourage habits in students which will help them, individually and/or collectively. Then we can add them to the kind of research findings described here.

How important is the students' motivation?

One of the most successful language learning experiences we know about took place towards the end of the Second World War when the American military needed to train their personnel in the languages of the countries they would have to administer and/or deal with. In short intensive courses, the students learnt fantastically fast. Likewise in Britain, Air Force personnel were taken to Cambridge and taught Russian, for example, with enormous success.

Whatever we think of the teaching methods used – or the reasons for the language learning – the teachers and students in these cases had a number of things on their side: they were highly motivated, they really wanted to learn and they had powerful reasons for doing so – including, of course, a fear of failure.

The desire to learn can come from many causes. Perhaps the students love the subject or are simply interested to see what it is like. On the other hand, they may have a practical reason for their study: they want to learn an instrument so they can play in an orchestra, learn English so they can watch American TV or work with English people, study Tai Chi so that they can become fitter and more relaxed, or go to cookery classes so that they can prepare better meals.

Famous research carried out in the second half of the twentieth century by Gardner and Lambert suggested that students who felt most warmly about a language and who wanted to integrate into the culture of its speakers were more highly motivated (and learnt more successfully) than those who were only learning language as a means to an end (e.g. getting a better job). In other words *Integrative* motivation was more powerful than *Instrumental* motivation. But whatever kind of motivation students have, it is clear that highly motivated students do better than ones without any motivation at all.

If good learners are those that have a positive attitude towards their subject, what can we do if we get students who aren't like that? Will students whose motivation is only skin-deep be bad learners? Will people who are not extremely keen to learn automatically fail?

One of the main tasks for teachers is to provoke interest and involvement in the subject even when students are not initially interested in it. It is by their choice of topic, activity and linguistic content that they may be able to turn a class around. It is by their attitude to class participation, their conscientiousness, their humour and their seriousness that they may influence their students. It is by their own behaviour and enthusiasm that they may inspire.

Teachers are not, however, ultimately responsible for their students' motivation. They can only encourage by word and deed. Real motivation comes from within each individual.

Who is responsible for learning?

In many modern language institutes, a sizeable percentage of time is given over to 'self-study'. Typically, the institute will have a large room equipped with textbooks, exercises, tape and video recorders (with individual headphones), reference books such as dictionaries, grammars etc, fiction and non-fiction books and magazines. There will be a competent teacher on duty to offer help and advice, but the idea is that the students should go in to this 'self-access' centre and choose what they want to do based on their own interest and needs. They can decide whether they want to go to the centre in other words, and, once there, they can take charge, do what they think is best, *take responsibility* for their own learning.

The underlying philosophy behind self-access centres is that students who are prepared to take such responsibility for their own learning (by studying in their own time, doing homework, thinking carefully about what would be best for them) are good learners. Good learners, in other words, don't just wait to be taught.

Of course, not every school has self-access facilities. They are expensive to set up and demand space and time. But the principle – that learners should take charge of their learning – is one that we need to promote with or without such physical resources. Students need to be aware that we cannot teach them English unless they themselves are prepared to take some of the strain. Learning is a partnership between teachers and students.

This message may be difficult for some students from certain educational backgrounds and cultures who have been led to believe that it is the teacher's job to provide learning. In such cases, teachers will not be successful if they merely try to impose a pattern of learner independence. In such cases, it is much better to start very gradually with a piece of homework, for example, or some solowork in class where individual students have to investigate a grammar issue or solve a reading puzzle on their own. As students get used to working things out for themselves and/or doing work at home, so they can gradually start to take their own decisions about learning.

Getting students to do various kinds of homework like written exercises, compositions or study is the best way to encourage student autonomy. What is important is that teachers should choose the right kind of task for the students. It should be within their grasp, and not take up too much of their time – or occupy too little of it by being trivial. Even more importantly than this, teachers should follow up homework when they say they are going to, imposing the same deadlines upon themselves as they do on their students.

As teachers, then, it is up to us to encourage students to take charge of their learning by guiding them in their choice of work either at home or in self-access centres (if they exist) and by being available to discuss individual plans of study. The most important thing, however, is to be sensitive to their own expectations of learning and act accordingly.

What characteristics do good classroom learners share?

Inside the classroom, some learners seem to take advantage of what's going on more than others. It looks as if they are more engaged with the process of learning than their colleagues. Teachers are aware of this too. They will frequently say that successful students possess some or all of the following characteristics.

A willingness to listen: good learners listen to what's going on – not just in the sense of paying attention, but also in terms of really listening to the English that is being used, soaking it up with eagerness and intelligence.

A willingness to experiment: many good learners are not afraid to 'have a go'. They are prepared to take risks, to try things out and see how it works. Of course, not all successful language learners are extroverts, but the urge to use the language (loudly or quietly) is an important one.

A willingness to ask questions: although some teachers can become irritated by students who are constantly asking difficult (and sometimes irrelevant) questions, the urge to find out why is part of a successful learner's equipment. Good teachers frequently invite students to ask if they don't understand something. Good learners do this, judging when it is appropriate to do so and when it is not.

A willingness to think about how to learn: good learners bring or invent their own study skills when they come to a lesson (and/or when they study on their own). They think about the best way to write vocabulary in their own wordbooks, for example, the best way to read a text (slowly, translating every word? or quickly, trying to get a general understanding?), the best method of drafting and re-drafting a piece of writing.

A willingness to accept correction: good learners are prepared to be corrected if it helps them. They are keen to get feedback from the teacher and act upon what they are told. But this only works where teachers are able to offer constructive criticism rather than castigating them for being wrong. Giving feedback involves praising students for things they do well, and offering them the ability to do things better where they were less successful. It involves teachers in judging their students' responses to correction so that they can act accordingly.

If these are good learner qualities, then it is part of a teacher's job to encourage them by creating an atmosphere which shows students that their experimentation and questions are welcome (within reason). Teachers can spend some time discussing how to learn with them, guiding them towards their own best methods of study.

What's special about teaching adults?

Perhaps the greatest difference between adults and younger ages is that the former come to lessons with a long history of learning experience. They will usually have gone through at least ten years of schooling and may then have gone on to study at a higher level. Those learning experiences – both bad and good – will have helped them to form strong opinions about how

10

teaching and learning should be carried out. They also come with their own record of success or failure. Those who underachieved at school may subconsciously assume that they are going to fail again; those who were school successes may believe that learning English will be easy.

Adolescents (and to a lesser extent children) have their own histories too. Each failure predisposes them to more failure, each success provokes the hope of more success. But the younger the student the less likely it is that these educational histories are fixed.

Adults are frequently more nervous of learning than younger pupils are. The potential for losing face becomes greater the older you get. Adolescents dislike being made to look foolish in front of their classmates too, but there are probably other things which make them vulnerable in this way rather than an inability to learn (English). Older students, on the other hand, who are coming back to the classroom after a long absence, may have a high degree of anxiety about the process of learning itself.

One of the recurring nightmares for teachers of adolescents is losing control: the lesson that slips away from them, that they can't control because the students don't like the subject, each other, the teacher or the school – or sometimes just because they feel like it. Adults can be disruptive and exhausting too. They may not do it in the same way as younger learners, but teachers of this age group will have experiences of students who spend the lesson talking to their neighbours when the teacher is trying to focus their attention or who disagree vocally with much of what the teacher is saying. They arrive in class late and fail to do any homework. And, whatever the causes of this behaviour, a problem is created.

Nevertheless, adults as a group have much to recommend them. They bring life experience into the classroom which younger learners do not necessarily have. They may well have a view of the importance of learning which makes them stick to a course of study in a specifically adult way. The attention span that cooperative adults can offer is almost certainly greater than that of children and adolescents. Lastly, teachers of adults are much less likely to have to deal with ongoing daily discipline problems than secondary school teachers are. They can expect more immediate cooperation from the majority of their students.

Whereas in primary schools much learning takes place through play and knowledge gathering is done through games, songs and puzzles, adults, on the other hand, do not necessarily need their learning to be camouflaged, dressed up in quite the same way. If they can see the point of learning – and if we are able to explain the reason why we are asking them to do things to their satisfaction – we do not have to play games or sing songs to get their cooperation.

It is, of course, possible for adults to suffer from boredom in class, especially when they are studying on a full-time course and/or have studied in the same kind of class for a long time. Such people may respond well to lessons that are entertaining and which use enjoyable activities to facilitate language learning. We won't want to treat them like children, but some of them might, nevertheless, respond well to a lighter style of learning which does, indeed, involve quizzes, puzzles and the study of contemporary songs.

Good teachers are able to balance the serious study of English with the more entertaining activities that they think their students sometimes need. By watching their classes and asking their students what they think and feel, they can select a judicious blend of activity and style.

What are the different levels?

Teachers of English generally make three basic level distinctions: *beginner*, *intermediate* and *advanced* (though exactly what these terms mean often depends where you work and what textbook (if any) you are using). Broadly, however, *beginners* are those who don't know any English and *advanced* students are those whose level of English is competent, allowing them to read unsimplified fact and fiction and communicate fluently with native speakers. Between these two extremes, *intermediate* suggests a basic competence in speaking and writing and an ability to comprehend fairly straightforward listening and reading.

Between these levels, other descriptive terms are used too. A distinction is made between *beginners* and *false beginners* to reflect the fact that some adults start a beginners' course having heard virtually no English, whereas many others can't really use any English but actually know quite a lot which can be quickly activated; they're not real beginners. *Elementary* students are no longer beginners and are able to communicate in a basic way. They can string some sentences together, construct a simple story or take part in predictable spoken interactions. However, they have not yet achieved intermediate competence which involves greater fluency and general comprehension of some general authentic English: there are still areas of knowledge – tense structures, noun phrase construction, vocabulary use etc. – which elementary students have not come across. *Upper intermediate* students, on the other hand, have the competence of intermediate students plus an extended knowledge of grammatical construction and skill use. However, they may not have achieved the accuracy or depth of knowledge which their advanced colleagues have acquired. The following diagram shows the labels which are frequently used to describe different levels.

Although each student is an individual, it is nevertheless possible to make some broad generalisations about the different levels.

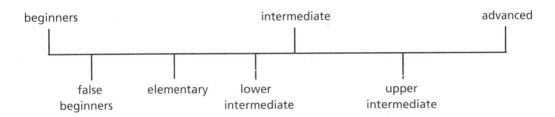

Terms for student levels

Beginners: success is easy to see at this level, and easy for the teacher to arrange. But then so is failure! Some adult beginners find that language learning is more stressful than they expected and reluctantly give up. However, if things are going well, teaching beginners can be incredibly stimulating – and great fun. It may be restricting for the teacher, but the pleasure of being able to see your part in your students' success is invigorating.

Intermediate students: success is not so easy to perceive here. Intermediate students have already achieved a lot. Gone are the days when they could observe their progress almost daily. Sometimes, it may seem to them, they don't improve that much or that fast anymore. We often call this the *plateau* effect, and the teacher has to make strenuous attempts to show students what they still need to learn without being discouraging. One of the ways of doing this is to make the tasks we give them more challenging and to get them to analyse language more thoroughly. We need to help them to set clear goals for themselves so that they have something to measure their achievement by.

Advanced students: they already know a lot of English. There is still the danger of the plateau effect (even if the plateau itself is higher up) so we have to create a classroom culture where learning is not seen as learning a language little-bit-by-little-bit. At the advanced level, we need to be able to show students what still has to be done and we need to provide good clear evidence of progress. We can do this through a concentration not so much on grammatical accuracy, but on style and perceptions of appropriacy, connotation and inference, helping students to use language with more subtlety. It is at this level, especially, that we have to encourage students to take more and more responsibility for their own learning.

How should we teach the different levels?

Although many activities can clearly be used at more than one level ('designing' newspaper front pages, writing radio commercials etc.), there are some which are obviously more appropriate for beginners, for example, pronunciation practice of /ə/, simple introduction dialogues, while there are others which are more appropriate for advanced students, such as discursive essay writing or formal debating.

One obvious difference in the way we teach different levels is language. Beginners need to be exposed to fairly simple language which they can understand. In their language work, they may get pleasure (and good learning) from concentrating on straightforward questions like 'What's your name?', 'What's your telephone number?', 'Hello', 'Goodbye' etc. Intermediate students know all this language already and so we will not ask them to concentrate on it.

The level of language also affects the teacher's behaviour. At beginner levels, the need for us to rough-tune our speech is very great: we can exaggerate our voice tone and gesture to help us to get our meaning across. But at higher levels, such extreme behaviour is not so important. Indeed, it will probably come across to the students as patronising.

The activities we offer students often depend on their language level too. For beginners, we will not suggest abstract discussions. For advanced students, a drill (with repetition in chorus) focusing on simple past tense questions will almost certainly be inappropriate. Where a simple role-play with ordinary information questions ('What time does the next train to London leave?', 'What's the platform for the London train?' etc.) may be a good target for beginners to aim at, the focus for advanced students will have to be richer and more subtle, for example, 'What's the best way to persuade someone of your opinion in an argument?', 'How can we structure writing to hold the reader's attention?', 'What different devices do English speakers use to give emphasis to the bits of information they want you to notice?'

Teachers react both overtly and subconsciously to different levels. The material they use – and the activities they get students to engage in – reflect the unique needs of those students at the level they have reached.

Conclusions

In this chapter we have
- looked at what makes a good learner and talked about how learners differ from each other in age and level.
- discussed the issue of motivation – the students' desire to learn. We have said that, even where it isn't present, positive experiences in the classroom may change the students' attitude – for the better.
- stressed that good learners take some of the responsibility for learning themselves. Whilst being sensitive to their own educational and cultural background, we should try and encourage the practice of self-study.
- said that good learners are willing to experiment, listen, ask questions and think about how to learn. This implies the desirability of using appropriate study skills.
- described adult learners. We have said that, like adolescents, they can be disruptive (though in different ways), that they can be quite nervous about learning but that they also have more world knowledge and a greater tolerance for 'serious' learning.
- described some of the different levels which students can reach. We have seen that in the choice of language and activities, what is important is to choose appropriately. What is suitable for beginners may not be so popular for advanced students.

Looking ahead

- In Chapters 6–10, the intended student level (elementary, intermediate, advanced etc.) for each activity will be suggested.
- Chapter 12 on lesson planning will draw together many of the issues about matching activities to the appropriate age group or level made in this chapter.
- However 'good' or 'bad' the students are, the teacher needs to *manage* the classroom, both in terms of his or her own presence and in the way the classroom is physically organised. That is what we look at in the next chapter.

How to manage teaching and learning

3

- How should teachers use their physical presence in class?
- How should teachers use their voices in class?
- How should teachers mark the stages of a lesson?
- What's the best seating arrangement for a class?
- What different student groupings can teachers use?
- How can teachers evaluate the success or failure of their lessons?

How should teachers use their physical presence in class?

As we saw from the comment about a teacher's clothes (page 3), the teacher's physical presence plays a large part in his or her management of the classroom environment. And it's not just appearance either. The way the teacher moves, how he or she stands, how physically demonstrative he or she is – all these play their part in the effective management of a class.

All teachers, like all people, have their own physical characteristics and habits, and they will take these into the classroom with them. But there are a number of issues to consider which are not just idiosyncratic and which have a direct bearing on the students' perception of us.

Proximity: teachers should consider how close they want to be to the students they are working with. Some students resent it if the distance between them and the teacher is too small. For others, on the other hand, distance is a sign of coldness. Teachers should be conscious of their proximity and, in assessing their students' reactions to what is happening in the classroom, they should take this into account.

Appropriacy: deciding how closely you should work with students is a matter of appropriacy. So is the general way in which teachers sit or stand in classrooms. Many teachers create an extremely friendly atmosphere by crouching down when they work with students in pairs. In this way, they are at the same level as their seated students. However, some students find this informality worrying. Some teachers are even happy to sit on the floor, and in certain situations this may be appropriate. But in others it may well lead to a situation where students are put off from concentrating.

All the positions teachers take – sitting on the edge of tables, standing behind a lectern, standing on a raised dais etc. – make strong statements about the kind of person the teacher is. It is important, therefore, to consider what kind of effect such physical behaviour has so that we can behave in a way which is appropriate to the students we have and the relationship we wish to create with them. If we want to manage a class effectively, such a relationship is crucial.

Movement: some teachers tend to spend most of their class time in one place – at the front of the class, for example, or to the side, or in the middle. Others spend a great deal of time walking from side to side, or striding up and down the aisles between the chairs. Although this, again, is to some extent a matter of personal preference, it is worth remembering that motionless teachers can bore students, whilst teachers who are constantly in motion can turn their students into tennis-match spectators, their heads moving from side to side until they become exhausted.

Most successful teachers move around the classroom to some extent. That way they can retain their students' interest (if they are leading an activity) or work more closely with smaller groups (when they go to help a pair or group).

How much a teacher moves around in the classroom, then, will depend on his or her personal style, where he or she feels most comfortable for the management of the class, how she or he feels it easiest to manage the classroom effectively, and whether or not he or she wants to work with smaller groups.

Contact: much of what we have said is about the issue of contact. How can teachers make contact with students? How close should that contact be?

In order to manage a class successfully, the teacher has to be aware of what students are doing and, where possible, how they are feeling. This means watching and listening just as carefully as teaching. It means being able to move around the class, getting the level of proximity right. It means making eye contact with students (provided that this is not culturally inappropriate), listening to what they have said and responding appropriately.

It is almost impossible to help students to learn a language in a classroom setting without making contact with them. The exact nature of this contact will vary from teacher to teacher and from class to class.

The teacher's physical approach and personality in the class is one aspect of class management to consider. Another is one of the teacher's chief tools: the voice.

How should teachers use their voices in class?

Perhaps the teacher's most important instrument is the voice. How we speak and what our voice sounds like have a crucial impact on classes. When considering the use of the voice in the management of teaching there are three issues to think about.

Audibility: clearly, teachers need to be audible. They must be sure that the students at the back of the class can hear them just as well as those at the front. But audibility cannot be divorced from voice quality: a rasping shout is always unpleasant.

Teachers do not have to shout to be audible. In fact, in most classrooms, there is a danger of the teacher's voice being too loud. Good teachers try to get this balance between audibility and volume just right.

Variety: it is important for teachers to vary the quality of their voices – and the volume they speak at – depending on the type of lesson and the type of activity. So the kind of voice you use to give instructions or introduce a new activity will be different from the voice which is most appropriate for conversation or an informal exchange of views or information.

In one particular situation, teachers often use very loud voices, and that is when they want students to be quiet or stop doing something (see the next section). But it is worth pointing out that speaking quietly is often just as effective a way of getting the students' attention since, when they realise that you are talking, they will want to stop and listen in case you are saying something important or interesting. However, for teachers who almost never raise their voices, the occasional shouted interjection may have an extremely dramatic effect, and this can sometimes be beneficial.

Conservation: just like opera singers, teachers have to take great care of their voices. It is important that they breathe correctly from the diaphragm so that they don't strain their larynxes. It is important that they vary their voices throughout a day, avoiding shouting wherever possible, so that they can conserve their vocal energy. Conserving the voice is one thing teachers will want to take into account when planning a day's or a week's work.

How should teachers mark the stages of a lesson?

If, as we said in Chapter 1, the teacher needs to provide variety, then clearly he or she will have to include different stages in his or her lessons.

When he or she arrives in the classroom, the teacher needs to start the lesson off. Where possible and appropriate, he or she needs to tell the students what they will be doing or, in a different kind of lesson, needs to discuss with them what they are hoping to achieve.

Teachers do not always explain exactly what they are going to do, however, since they sometimes want to maintain an element of surprise. But even in such cases, a clear start to the lesson is necessary just as a play often starts with the rise of a curtain, or a visit to the doctor starts when he or she asks you, 'Now then, what seems to be the problem?' or 'How can I help you?'

When an activity has finished and/or another one is about to start, it helps if teachers make this clear through the way they behave and the things they say. It helps students if they are made clearly aware of the end of something and the beginning of what is coming next. Frequently, teachers need to re-focus the students' attention, or point it in some new direction.

In order for such changes of direction to be effective, the teacher first needs to get the students' attention. This can sometimes be difficult, especially when teachers try to draw a speaking activity to a conclusion, or when students are working in groups. Some teachers clap their hands to get students' attention. Some speak loudly, saying things like, 'Thank you ... now can I have your attention please?' or 'OK ... thanks ... let's all face the front shall we?' Another method is for the teacher to raise his or her hand. When individual students see this, they raise their hands briefly in reply to indicate that they are now going to be quiet and wait for the next stage.

Finally, when an activity or a lesson has finished, it helps if the teacher is able to provide some kind of closure – a summary of what has happened, perhaps, or a prediction of what will take place in the next lesson. Sometimes, teachers find themselves in the middle of something when the bell goes, but this is unfortunate, because it leaves unfinished business behind, and a sense of incompleteness. It is much better to round the lesson off successfully.

What's the best seating arrangement for a class?

In many classrooms around the world students sit in orderly rows. Sometimes, their chairs have little wooden palettes on one of the arms as surfaces to write on. Sometimes, the students will have desks in front of them. It is not unknown to find the chairs bolted to the floor. At the front of such classrooms, frequently on a raised platform (so that all the students can see them), stand the teachers. In contrast, there are other institutions where you can find students sitting in a large circle around the walls of the classroom. Or you may see small groups of them working in different parts of the room. Sometimes, they are arranged in a horseshoe shape around the teacher. Sometimes, it is not immediately obvious who the teacher is.

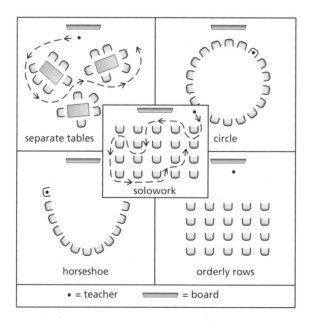

Different seating arrangements in class

Clearly, we are seeing a number of different approaches in the different arrangements of chairs and tables and this raises a number of questions. Are schools which use a variety of seating plans progressive or merely modish, for example? Is there something intrinsically superior about rigid seating arrangements – or are such classrooms the product of traditional orthodoxy? Is one kind of seating arrangement better than another? What are the advantages of each? The following discusses these various arrangements.

Orderly rows: when the students sit in rows in classrooms, there are obvious advantages. It means that the teacher has a clear view of all the students and the students can all see the teacher – in whose direction they are facing. It makes lecturing easy, enabling the teacher to maintain eye contact with the people he or she is talking to. It also makes discipline easier since it is more difficult to be disruptive when you are sitting in a row. If there are aisles in the classroom, the teacher can easily walk up and down making more personal contact with individual students and watching what they are doing.

Orderly rows imply teachers working with the whole class. Some activities are especially suited to this kind of organisation: explaining a grammar point, watching a video, using the board, demonstrating text organisation on an overhead transparency which shows a paragraph, for example. It is also useful when students are involved in certain kinds of language practice (as we shall see in Chapter 6). If all the students are focused on a task, the whole class gets the same messages.

When teachers are working with the whole class sitting in orderly rows, it is vitally important to make sure that they remain in contact with the students and that they keep everyone involved. So, if they are asking questions to the class, they must remember to ask students at the back, the quiet ones perhaps, rather than just the ones nearest them. They must move round so that they can see all the students to gauge their reactions to what's going on.

One trick that many teachers use is to keep their students guessing. Especially where teachers need to ask individual students questions, it is important that they should not do so in order, student after student, line by line. That way, the procedure becomes very tedious and the students know when they are going to be asked and, once this has happened, that they are not going to be asked again. It is much better to ask students from all parts of the room in apparently random order. It keeps everyone on their toes!

In many classrooms of the world, teachers are faced with classes of anywhere between 40 and 200 students at a time. In such circumstances, orderly rows may well be the best or only solution.

Circles and horseshoes: in smaller classes, many teachers and students prefer circles or horseshoes. In a horseshoe, the teacher will probably be at the open end of the arrangement since that may well be where the board, overhead projector and/or tape recorder are situated. In a circle, the teacher's position – where the board is situated – is less dominating.

Classes which are arranged in a circle make quite a strong statement about what the teacher and the students believe in. The Round Table in the legends about King Arthur was designed by him specially so that there would not be arguments about who was more important than who – and that included the King himself when they were in a meeting. So it is in classrooms. With all the people in the room sitting in a circle, there is a far greater feeling of equality than when the teacher stays out at the front. This may not be quite so true of the horseshoe shape where the teacher is often located in a central position, but even here the teacher has a much greater opportunity to get close to the students.

If, therefore, teachers believe in lowering the barriers between themselves and their students, this kind of seating arrangement will help. There are other advantages too, chief among which is the fact that all the students can see each other. In an 'orderly row' classroom, you have to turn round – that is, away from the teacher – if you want to make eye contact with someone behind you. In a circle or a horseshoe, no such disruption is necessary. The classroom is thus a more intimate place and the potential for students to share feelings and information through talking, eye contact or expressive body movements (eyebrow-raising, shoulder-shrugging etc.) is far greater.

Separate tables: Even circles and horseshoes seem rather formal compared to classes where students are seated in small groups at individual tables. In such classrooms, you might see the teacher walking around checking the students' work and helping out if they are having difficulties – prompting the students at this table, or explaining something to the students at the table in the corner.

When students sit in small groups at individual tables, the atmosphere in the class is much less hierarchical than in other arrangements. It is much easier for the teacher to work at one table while the others get on with their own work. It feels less like teacher and students and more like responsible adults getting on with the business of learning.

However, this arrangement is not without its own problems. In the first place, students may not always want to be with the same colleagues: indeed, their preferences may change over time. Secondly, it makes 'whole-class' teaching more difficult, since the students are more diffuse and separated.

The way students sit says a lot about the style of the teacher or the institution where the lessons take place. Many teachers would like to re-arrange their classes so that they are not always faced with rows and rows of bored faces. Even where this is physically impossible – in terms of furniture, for example – there are things they can do to achieve this as we shall see in the next section.

What different student groupings can teachers use?

Whatever the seating arrangements in a classroom, students can be organised in different ways: they can work as a whole class, in groups, in pairs, or individually.

Whole class: as we have seen, there are many occasions when a teacher working with the class as a whole is the best type of classroom organisation. However, this does not always mean the class sitting in orderly rows; whatever the seating arrangement, the teacher can have the students focus on him or her and the task in hand.

Groupwork and pairwork: these have become increasingly popular in language teaching since they are seen to have many advantages. Groupwork is a cooperative activity: five students, perhaps, discussing a topic, doing a role-play or solving a problem. In groups, students tend to participate more equally, and they are also more able to experiment and use the language than they are in a whole-class arrangement.

Pairwork has many of the same advantages. It is mathematically attractive if nothing else; the moment students get into pairs and start working on a problem or talking about something, many more of them will be doing the activity than if the teacher was working with the whole class, where only one student talks at a time.

Both pairwork and groupwork give the students chances for greater independence. Because they are working together without the teacher controlling every move, they take some of their own learning decisions, they decide what language to use to complete a certain task, and they can work without the pressure of the whole class listening to what they are doing. Decisions are cooperatively arrived at, responsibilities are shared.

The other great advantage of groupwork and pairwork (but especially groupwork) is that they give the teacher the opportunity to work with individual students. While groups A and C are doing one task, the teacher can spend some time with Group B who need special attention.

Neither groupwork nor pairwork are without their problems. As with 'separate table' seating, students may not like the people they are grouped or paired with. In any one group or pair, one student may dominate while the others stay silent. In difficult classes, groupwork may encourage students to be more disruptive than they would be in a whole-class setting, and, especially in a class where students share the same first language, they may revert to their first language, rather than English, when the teacher is not working with them.

Apart from groupwork and pairwork, the other alternative to whole-class teaching is solowork.

Solowork: this can have many advantages: it allows students to work at their own speed, allows them thinking time, allows them, in short, to be individuals. It often provides welcome relief from the group-centred nature of much language teaching. For the time that solowork takes place, students can relax their public faces and go back to considering their own individual needs and progress.

How much teachers use groupwork, pairwork or solowork depends to a large extent on teacher style and student preferences. Do the students actually enjoy pairwork? What do they get out of it? Do the advantages of groupwork – cooperation, involvement, autonomy – outweigh the advantages of whole-class grouping – clarity, dramatic potential, teacher control? Do the students work conscientiously during solowork sessions?

Good teachers are able to use different class groupings for different activities. While they do this, they will monitor which is more successful and for what, so that they can always seek to be more effective.

How can teachers evaluate the success or failure of their lessons?

All teachers, whether at the start of their careers or after some years of teaching, need to be able to try out new activities and techniques. It is important to be open to such new ideas and take them into the classroom.

But such experimentation will be of little use unless we can then evaluate these activities. Were they successful? Did the students enjoy them? Did they learn anything from them? How could the activities be changed to make them more effective next time?

One way of getting feedback is to ask students simple questions such as 'Did you like that exercise? Did you find it useful?' and see what they say. But not all students will discuss topics like this openly in class. It may be better to ask them to write their answers down and hand them in.

Another way of getting reactions to new techniques is to invite a colleague into the classroom and ask him or her to observe what happens and make suggestions afterwards. The lesson could also be videoed.

In general, it is a good idea to get students' reactions to lessons, and their aspirations about them, clearly stated. Many teachers encourage students to say what they feel about the lessons and how they think the course is going. The simplest way to do this is to ask students once every fortnight, for example, to write down two things they want more of and two things they want less of. The answers you get may prove a fruitful place to start a discussion, and you will then be able to modify what happens in class, if you think it appropriate, in the light of your students' feelings. Such modifications will greatly enhance the teacher's ability to manage the class.

Good teacher managers also need to assess how well their students are progressing. This can be done through a variety of measures including homework assignments, speaking activities where the teacher scores the participation of each student, and frequent small progress tests. Good teachers keep a record of their students' achievements so that they are always aware of how they are getting on. Only if teachers keep such kinds of progress records can they begin to see when teaching and learning has or has not been successful.

Conclusions

In this chapter we have
- discussed the teacher's physical presence, saying that we should pay attention to our proximity to the students, think about how much we move around the class, and consider the appropriacy of our behaviour in general.
- said that teachers need to make contact with their students, especially eye contact.
- discussed the fact that teachers need to be clearly audible without

shouting in a disagreeable way and stressed the need for variety in the way teachers use their voices. Different activities call for different voices, and the varied use of the voice makes for more interesting classes.

- mentioned that it is important for teachers to conserve their voices, perhaps their most important instrument.
- emphasised that teachers need to mark stages and changes of activity clearly so that students know what's going on. We said that successful teachers knew how to start classes and also how to close them so that there was a feeling of completeness.
- looked at different ways of arranging a class physically, from orderly rows to separate tables.
- discussed the uses of 'orderly row' classrooms and said that teachers need to keep in touch with what's going on and involve all the students in such a situation.
- suggested that circles, horseshoes, and, especially, separate tables make a class less regimented and teacher-dominated, whilst recognising that rows have their uses, and that the other arrangements are not without disadvantages.
- looked at the way teachers group students: whole class, groupwork, pairwork and solowork. We have stressed the advantages of groupwork and pairwork and looked at times when solowork comes as a great relief to students. Whole-class teaching is extremely beneficial in certain circumstances too.
- said that teachers need to try out new techniques and that, crucially, they need to evaluate them too. In particular, they need to be able to find out whether the students found them useful and/or enjoyable. We showed ways of doing this.
- finished by suggesting that teachers can use a variety of means to keep track of their students' progress – an important part of class management.

Looking ahead

- In many of the activities in Chapters 6–10, we will be suggesting the use of groups or pairs. Many of these activities will also work just as well if not better with varying seating arrangements of the kinds we have discussed here.
- When considering lesson planning in Chapter 12, issues of variety, marking stages, seating, groupings etc. will be of vital importance.
- For all the suggested activities in Chapters 6–10 (and in Chapter 11 about using textbooks) it will be vital for the teacher to evaluate how successful the activity has been.
- In Chapter 13 *What if?* we will look at what to do if students become disruptive – a major management issue.
- The next chapter suggests a model for teachers to follow and briefly discusses other models which have influenced the practice of English language teaching.

How to describe learning and teaching

- What do we know about language learning?
- What elements are necessary for successful language learning in classrooms?
- How do the three elements of *ESA* fit together in lesson sequences?
- What teaching models have influenced current teaching practice?

What do we know about language learning?

Outside the context of any classroom, all children who are repeatedly exposed to a language will in normal circumstances learn it. They do this unconsciously – rather than as a form of study.

Most adults can learn a language without studying it, providing they are in the right kind of contact with it. Though they may have more trouble with pronunciation and grammar than younger learners, they may still be able to communicate fluently.

However, not all adults who come into contact with a foreign language learn it. They might not want to. Perhaps the language they come into contact with is, in their view, just too complex for them. Perhaps, they don't hear or see enough of it or have sufficient opportunities to try it out.

Children and adults who do acquire language successfully outside the classroom seem to share certain similarities in their learning experiences. First of all, they are usually exposed to language which they more or less understand even if they can't produce the same language spontaneously themselves. Secondly, they are motivated to learn the language in order to be able to communicate. And finally, they have opportunities to use the language they are learning, thus giving themselves chances to flex their linguistic muscles – and check their own progress and abilities.

Babies and children get endless exposure to their first language coupled with emotional support. Adults living in a foreign country get continual exposure to the language at various different levels and can get help from the surrounding language speakers.

All these features of natural language acquisition can be difficult to replicate in the classroom, but there are elements which we should try to imitate.

What elements are necessary for successful language learning in classrooms?

Classroom students don't usually get the same kind of exposure or encouragement as those who – at whatever age – are 'picking up' the language. But that does not mean they cannot learn a language if the right conditions apply. Like language learners outside schools, they will need to be motivated, be exposed to language, and given chances to use it. We can therefore say what elements need to be present in a language classroom to help students learn effectively. We will call these elements *'ESA'*, three elements which will be present in all – or almost all – classes. They are:

Engage: this is the point in a teaching sequence where teachers try to arouse the students' interest, thus involving their emotions.

Most people can remember lessons at school which were uninvolving and where they 'switched off' from what was being taught them. Frequently, this was because they were bored, because they were not emotionally engaged with what was going on. Such lessons can be contrasted with lessons where they were amused, moved, stimulated or challenged. It seems quite clear that those lessons involved not only more 'fun', but also better learning.

Activities and materials which frequently *Engage* students include: games (depending on age and type), music, discussions (when handled challengingly), stimulating pictures, dramatic stories, amusing anecdotes etc. But even where such activities and materials are not used, teachers will want to ensure that their students *Engage* with the topic, exercise or language they are going to be dealing with. They will ask students what they think of a topic before asking them to read about it, for example. They will look at the picture of a person and be asked to guess what their occupation is before they listen to that person on tape, they will have been stimulated by the fact that the teacher (who normally dresses very formally and always stays in the same place in class) suddenly arrives in class dressed casually and moves around the room with unaccustomed ease, and so on.

When students are *Engaged*, they learn better than when they are partly or wholly disengaged!

Study: *Study* activities are those where the students are asked to focus in on language (or information) and how it is constructed. They range from the study and practice of a single sound to an investigation of how a writer achieves a particular effect in a long text; from an examination and practice of a verb tense to the study of a transcript of informal speech to discuss spoken style.

Students can study in a variety of different styles: the teacher can explain grammar, they can study language evidence to discover grammar for themselves, they can work in groups studying a reading text or vocabulary. But whatever the style, *Study* means any stage at which the construction of language is the main focus.

Some typical areas for *Study* might be the study and practice of the vowel sound in 'ship' and 'sheep' (e.g. 'ch<u>i</u>p, ch<u>ea</u>p, d<u>i</u>p, d<u>ee</u>p, b<u>i</u>t, b<u>ea</u>t' etc.), the study and practice of the third person singular of the present simple ('He sleeps, She laughs, It works' etc), the study and practice of inviting patterns ('Would you like to come to the cinema/to a concert?' etc.), the study and practice of the way we use pronouns in written discourse (e.g. 'A man entered a house in Brixton. <u>He</u> was tall with an unusual hat. <u>It</u> was multicoloured ...' etc.), the study and practice of paragraph organisation (topic sentence, development, conclusion) or of the rules for using 'make' and 'do'.

Successful language learning in a classroom depends on a judicious blend of subconscious language acquisition (through listening and reading, for example) and the kind of *Study* activities we have looked at here.

Activate: this element describes exercises and activities which are designed to get students using language as freely and 'communicatively' as they can. The objective for the students is not to focus on language construction and/or practise specific bits of language (grammar patterns, particular vocabulary items or functions) but for them to use all and any language which may be appropriate for a given situation or topic. Thus, *Activate* exercises offer students a chance to try out real language use with little or no restriction – a kind of rehearsal for the real world.

Typical *Activate* exercises include role-plays (where students act out, as realistically as possible, an exchange between a travel agent and a client, for example), advertisement design (where students write and then record a radio commercial, for example), debates and discussions, 'Describe and Draw' (where one student tries to get another to draw a picture without that other student being able to see the original), story and poem writing, writing in groups etc.

If students do not have a chance to *Activate* their knowledge in the safety of a classroom, they may find transferring language acquisition and study into language use in the real world far more problematical.

These *ESA* elements need to be present in most lessons or teaching sequences. Whether the main focus of the lesson is a piece of grammar (in which case there will be opportunities for *Study* and *Activation*), or whether the focus is on reading (where there may be a lot of *Activation* of language knowledge in the processing of the text, but where, at some stage, the students will also *Study* the construction of that text or the use of some language within it), students always need to be *Engaged*, if possible, so that they can get the maximum out of the learning experience. Most students will want to have *Studied* some aspect of language, however small or of short duration, during a lesson period.

There are some exceptions to this, of course, notably in classes where an *Activation* exercise takes up a lot of time, for example, with a debate or a role-play or a piece of extended writing. In such cases, teachers may not want to interrupt the flow of *Activation* with a *Study* stage. But they will want to use the exercise as a basis for previous or subsequent study of language aspects which are crucial to the activity. The same might be true of an extended *Study* period where chances for *Activation* are few. But, in both these cases, the only limitation is time. The missing elements will appear, only perhaps later.

The majority of teaching and learning at lower levels is not made up of such long activities, however. Instead, it is far more likely that there will be more than one *ESA* sequence in a given lesson sequence or period.

To say that the three elements need to be present does not mean they always have to take place in the same order. The last thing we want to do is bore our students by constantly offering them the same predictable learning patterns – as we discussed in Chapter 1. It is, instead, our responsibility to vary the sequences and content of our lessons, and the different *ESA* patterns that we are now going to describe show how this can be done.

How do the three elements of *ESA* fit together in lesson sequences?

One type of teaching sequence takes students in a straight line: first the teacher gets the class interested and *Engaged*, then they *Study* something and they then try to *Activate* it by putting it into production. Here is an example of such a 'Straight Arrows' sequence designed for elementary-level students.

1 **Engage:** students and teacher look at a picture or video of modern robots. They say what the robots are doing. They say why they like or don't like robots.
2 **Study:** the teacher shows students (the picture of) a particular robot. Students are introduced to 'can' and 'can't' (how they are pronounced and constructed) and say things like 'It can do maths' and 'It can't play the piano'. The teacher tries to make sure the sentences are pronounced correctly and that the students use accurate grammar.
3 **Activate:** students work in groups and design their own robot. They make a presentation to the class saying what their robot can and can't do.

We can represent this kind of lesson in the following way.

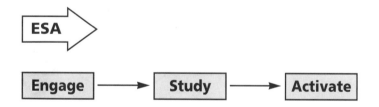

ESA Straight Arrows sequence

Straight Arrows lessons work very well for certain structures. The robot example above clearly shows how 'can' and 'can't' are constructed and how they are used. It gives students a chance to practise the language in a controlled way (during the *Study* phase) and then gives them the chance to *Activate* the 'new' language in an enjoyable way.

However, if we teach all our lessons like this, we may not be giving our students' own learning styles a fair chance. Such a procedure may work at lower levels for straightforward language, but it might not be so appropriate for more advanced learners with more complex language.

Thus, while there is nothing wrong with going in a straight line – for the right students at the right level learning the right language – it is not always appropriate. Instead, there are other possibilities for the sequence of the *ESA* elements. Here, for example, is a 'Boomerang' procedure.

1 **Engage:** students and teacher discuss issues surrounding job interviews. What makes a good interviewee? What sort of thing does the interviewer want to find out? The students get interested in the discussion.
2 **Activate:** the teacher describes an interview situation which the students are going to act out in a role-play. The students plan the kind of questions they are going to ask and the kind of answers they might want to give (not focusing on language construction etc., but treating it as a real-life task). They then role-play the interviews. While they are doing this, the teacher makes a note of English mistakes they make and difficulties they have.
3 **Study:** when the role-plays are over, the teacher works with the students on the grammar and vocabulary which caused them trouble during the role-play. They might compare their language with more correct usage and try to work out (discover) for themselves where they went wrong. They might do some controlled practice of the language.
4 **Activate:** some time later, students role-play another job interview, bringing in the knowledge they gained in the *Study* phase.

The diagram for boomerang lessons represents this procedure in the following way.

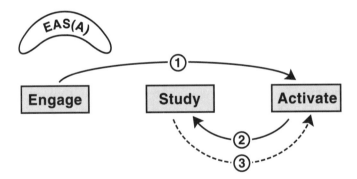

EAS(A) Boomerang sequence

In this sequence the teacher is answering the needs of the students. They are not taught language until and unless they have shown (in the *Activate* phase) that they have a need for it. In some ways, this makes much better sense because the connection between what students need to learn and what they are taught is more transparent. However, it places a greater burden on the teacher since he or she will have to be able to find good teaching material based on the (often unforeseen) problems thrown up at the *Activate* stage. It may also be more appropriate for students at intermediate and advanced levels since they have quite a lot of language available for them at the *Activate* stage.

The two procedures we've shown so far demonstrate two different approaches to language teaching. In straight arrows sequences the teacher knows what the students need and takes them logically to the point where they can *Activate* the knowledge which he or she has helped them to acquire. For the boomerang sequence, however, the teacher selects the task the students need to perform, but then waits for the boomerang to come back before deciding what they need to *Study*.

Many lessons aren't quite as clear-cut as this, however. Instead, they are a mixture of procedures and mini-procedures, a variety of short episodes building up to a whole. Here is an example of this kind of 'Patchwork' lesson.

1   **Engage:** students look at a picture of sunbathers and respond to it by commenting on the people and the activity they are taking part in. Maybe they look at each other's holiday photos etc.
2   **Activate:** students act out a dialogue between a doctor and a sunburn victim after a day at the beach.
3   **Activate:** students look at a text describing different people and the effects the sun has on their skin. They say how they feel about it. (The text is on page 75 in this book.)
4   **Study:** the teacher does vocabulary work on words such as 'pale, fair-skinned, freckles, tan' etc., ensuring that students understand the meaning, the hyphened compound nature of some of them, and that they are able to say them with the correct pronunciation in appropriate contexts.
5   **Activate:** students describe themselves or people they know in the same kind of ways as the reading text.
6   **Study:** the teacher focuses the students' attention on the relative clause construction used in the text (e.g. 'I'm the type of person who always burns', 'I'm the type of person who burns easily'). The use of the 'who' clause is discussed and students practise sentences saying things like 'They're the kind of people who enjoy movies' etc.
7   **Engage:** the teacher discusses advertisements with the students. What are they for? What different ways do they try to achieve their effect? What are the most effective ads the students can think of? Perhaps the teacher plays some radio commercials or puts some striking visual ads on an overhead projector.
8   **Activate:** the students write a radio commercial for a sunscreen. The teacher lets them record it using sound effects and music.

The patchwork diagram for this teaching sequence is shown on the next page.

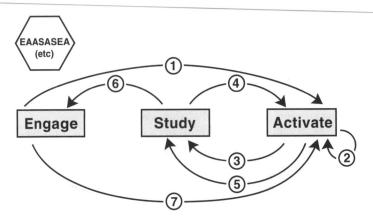

EAASASEA (etc.) Patchwork sequence

Such classes are very common, especially at intermediate and advanced levels. Not only do they probably reflect the way we learn – rather chaotically, not always in a straight line – but they also provide an appealing balance between *Study* and *Activation*, between language and topic. They also give the students the kind of flexibility we talked about in Chapter 1.

What teaching models have influenced current teaching practice?

For as long as people have been learning and teaching languages, there has been continual debate about how to describe the process and what the best ways of doing it are. Much current teaching practice is the direct result of such constructive argument.

There have been some traditional language learning techniques that have been used for many years. In more recent times, there have been five teaching models which have had a strong influence on classroom practice – and which teachers and trainers still refer to. They are Grammar-translation, Audio-lingualism, PPP, Task-Based Learning, and Communicative Language Teaching.

Grammar-translation: this was probably the most commonly used way of learning languages for hundreds of years – and it is still practised in many situations. Practitioners think that, by analysing the grammar and by finding equivalents between the students' language and the language to be studied, the students will learn how the foreign language is constructed.

It is certainly true that most language learners translate in their heads at various stages anyway, and we can learn a lot about a foreign language by comparing parts of it with parts of our own. But a concentration on grammar-translation stops the students from getting the kind of natural language input that will help them acquire language, and it often fails to give them opportunities to activate their language knowledge. The danger with grammar-translation, in other words, is that it teaches people about the language and doesn't really help them to learn the language itself.

Audio-lingualism: this is the name given to a language-teaching methodology based heavily on behaviourist theories of learning. These theories suggested that much learning is the result of habit formation through conditioning. As a result of this, audio-lingual classes concentrated on long repetition-drill stages, in which the teacher hoped that the students would acquire good language habits. By rewarding correct production during these repetition phases, students could be conditioned into learning the language.

Audio-lingualism (and behaviourism) went out of fashion because commentators from all sides argued that language learning was far more subtle than just the formation of habits. For example, students are soon able to say things they have never heard or practised before because all humans have the power to be creative in language based on the underlying knowledge they have acquired – including rules of construction, and a knowledge of when a certain kind or form of language is appropriate. Methodologists were also concerned that in audio-lingualism students were not exposed to real or realistic language.

However, it is interesting to note that drilling is still popular (in a far more limited way) during the *Study* phase, especially for low-level students – as some of the examples in Chapter 6 will show.

PPP: this stands for *Presentation*, *Practice* and *Production* and is similar to the straight arrows kind of lesson described above. In PPP classes or sequences, the teacher presents the context and situation for the language (e.g. describing a robot), and both explains and demonstrates the meaning and form of the new language ('can' and 'can't'). The students then practise making sentences with 'can' and 'can't' before going on to the production stage in which they talk more freely about themselves ('I can play the viola but I can't play the drums') or other people in the real world (e.g. 'My girlfriend can speak Spanish' etc.). As with straight arrows lessons, PPP is extremely effective for teaching simple language at lower levels. It becomes less appropriate when students already know a lot of language, and therefore don't need the same kind of marked presentation. A typical example of a basic PPP procedure is given in Chapter 6 (Example 1).

Task-Based Learning: here the emphasis is on the task rather than the language. For example, students might be encouraged to ask for information about train and bus timetables and to get the correct answers (that is the task). We give them the timetables and they then try and complete the task (after, perhaps, hearing someone else do it or asking for examples of the kind of language they might want to use). When they have completed the task, we can then, if necessary – and only if necessary – give them a bit of language study to clear up some of the problems they encountered while completing the task. Alternatively, we might ask them to write part of a guidebook for their area. When they have completed the task (which will involve finding facts, planning content and writing the brochure etc.), we can then read their efforts and do some language/writing study to help them to do better next time.

It will be noticed immediately that task-based learning sequences fit very neatly into our boomerang lesson description, where language *Activation* is the first goal and *Study* comes later if and when appropriate.

Communicative Language Teaching: this was a radical departure from the PPP-type lessons which had tended to dominate language teaching. Communicative Language Teaching has two main strands: the first is that language is not just bits of grammar, it also involves language *functions* such as *inviting*, *agreeing* and *disagreeing*, *suggesting* etc., which students should learn how to use. They also need to be aware of the need for appropriacy when talking and writing to people in terms of the kind of language they use (formal, informal, tentative, technical etc.).

The second strand of Communicative Language Teaching developed from the idea that if students get enough exposure to language and opportunities for its use – and if they are motivated – then language learning will take care of itself. In other words, the focus of much communicative language teaching became what we have called *Activation*, and *Study* tended to be downplayed to some extent.

Communicative Language Teaching has had a thoroughly beneficial effect since it reminded teachers that people learn languages not so that they 'know' them, but so that they can communicate. Giving students different kinds of language, pointing them to aspects of style and appropriacy, and above all giving them opportunities to try out real language within the classroom humanised what had sometimes been too regimented. Above all, it stressed the need for *Activation* and allowed us to consider boomerang- and patchwork-type lessons where before they tended to be less widely used.

Debate still continues, of course. Recent theory and practice have included: the introduction of *Discovery* activities (where students are asked to 'discover' facts about language for themselves rather than have the teacher or the book tell them – see example 4 in Chapter 6); the *Lexical Approach* in which it is argued that words and phrases are far better building blocks for language than grammatical structure; classroom stages being given new names to help us describe teaching and learning in different ways (e.g. see the reference to Scrivener on page 187); and the study of the difference between spoken and written language to suggest different activities and content on language courses. Further reading on all these is given in Appendix B on page 187.

Whichever way of describing language teachers prefer, the three elements described here – *Engage*, *Study* and *Activate* – are the basic building blocks for successful language teaching and learning. By using them in different and varied sequences, teachers will be doing their best to promote their students' success.

Conclusions   In this chapter we have

- talked about the elements necessary to learn language in the 'real' world: exposure, motivation and use.
- described the three elements necessary for successful teaching and learning in class: E (*Engage*), S (*Study*) and A (*Activate*).
- described three different lesson sequences which contain the *Engage*, *Study* and *Activate* elements. In straight arrows lessons, the order is *E-S-A*, but in boomerang lessons, teachers may move straight from an *Engage* stage to an *Activate* stage. *Study* can then be based on how well students performed (*E-A-S*). Patchwork classes mix the three elements in various different sequences (e.g. *E-A-A-S-A-S-E-A* ... etc.).
- talked about different models which people have used to describe teaching such as PPP (Presentation, Practice and Production), Task-Based Learning (which puts the task first and language study last) and Communicative Language Teaching (with its twin emphasis on appropriate language use and *Activation* methodology).
- seen how PPP is a form of straight arrows lessons, while Task-Based Learning is more like boomerang or patchwork sequences. We pointed out that Communicative Language Teaching was responsible for the modern emphasis on the *Activate* stages of lessons.
- mentioned, in passing, some of the issues which people are currently debating.
- pointed out that good teachers vary the *ESA* sequences they use with their students – to avoid monotony and offer a range of learning sequences. The three elements are always present, but in many and different combinations.

Looking ahead

- Chapter 6 *How to Teach Language* will look at many *Study*-focus activities (including a PPP-like sequence and a more 'discovery'-based procedure) and how such study sections fit into *ESA* sequences.
- In the chapters on reading, writing, listening and speaking (Chapters 7–10) we will see how the teaching examples can fit into different *ESA* procedures.
- Next, though, we are going to look at what teachers and students need to know about language.

5 How to describe language

- What does this chapter do?
- Sentence constructions
- Parts of speech
- Noun types
- Verb types
- Verb forms
- Pronouns
- Adjectives
- Adverbs
- Prepositions
- Articles
- Conjunctions and conditionals
- Forms and meanings
- Language functions
- Words together: collocation
- Speaking and writing
- Pronunciation

What does this chapter do? Both students and teachers need to know how to talk about language at various points during learning and teaching. This is not only so that teachers can explain and students come to understand, but also so that teachers know what's going wrong where and how to correct it. While it is perfectly possible to learn a language outside the classroom with no reference to the technical aspects of language, in classrooms with teachers it will help if all the participants are able to say how the sounds /b/ (as in 'berry') and /v/ (as in 'very') are made, why we don't say 'I have seen him yesterday', or what is wrong with 'childish crime' when we mean 'juvenile crime'.

In order to be able to talk about language, we need to know how to describe its various elements. In this chapter, we will therefore look at some fairly basic language descriptions and issues. However, it is important to realise that a short chapter can only scratch the surface of an extremely complex and challenging collection of different language issues. It can only be a basic beginning to a much much bigger area for investigation. It is intended only as an introduction to some of the terms and issues which teachers and students may need. Teachers must follow up the themes touched on here; indeed they need to have at least one of the grammar books mentioned in Appendix B on page 187 (or an equivalent) on their shelves so that they can learn and investigate further, and as a constant reference work during their teaching lives. In other words, this chapter only *introduces* concepts which teachers (and students) need to become familiar with and which they will then need to build on in their different ways and at different levels.

In order to work out some of the issues raised in this chapter, it will be a good idea to read about them in conjunction with the Task File for the chapter on pages 148–52. In doing the tasks, some of the issues will become clearer, some of the contrasts will becomes starker.

We will start by looking at a number of 'Grammar' issues.

Sentence constructions

One way of describing different kinds of sentences is to use the terms Subject, Object, Verb, Complement and Adverbial. Thus, a simple sentence such as 'The dog bit the man' contains a subject ('The dog'), a verb ('bit') and an object ('the man'). Other similar sentences can be 'He read the paper', 'She solved the problem', 'Columbus discovered America'. Verbs like these, with objects, are called *transitive*.

Complements: a complement is used with verbs like 'be', 'seem', 'look' etc. to give information about the subject. For example, the sentence 'She seems happy' contains a subject ('She'), a verb ('seems') and a complement ('happy'). Examples of other sentences with complements are 'They are Irish', 'He was a brilliant pianist', 'She was in a bad mood'.

Subject + verb only: some sentences are formed with only subjects and verbs (e.g. 'He laughed', 'They disagreed', 'It poured!'). Verbs such as these which can't take an object are called *intransitive*, e.g. 'laugh', 'disagree'. Some verbs can be either transitive or intransitive, e.g. 'She <u>opened</u> the door/The door <u>opened</u>'.

Two objects: there are two kinds of objects, direct and indirect. Direct objects refer to things or persons affected by the verb, e.g. 'He sang <u>a song</u>', 'Pizarro conquered <u>Peru</u>', 'She loved <u>him</u>'.

An indirect object refers to the person or thing that (in one grammarian's phrase) 'benefits' from the action, e.g. 'He sang <u>me</u> a song', 'She painted <u>him</u> a picture', 'I gave a ring <u>to my girlfriend</u>', 'Why should we pay taxes <u>to the government</u>?'.

Adverbial (phrases): adverbials or adverbial phrases complement the verb in the same way that a complement 'complements' the subject, e.g. 'He lived <u>in Paris</u>' (adverbial of place), 'They arrived <u>late/at night</u>' (adverbial of time), 'She sings <u>beautifully/like an angel</u>' (adverbial of manner).

Multi-clause sentences: all the sentences we have looked at so far are simple sentences, that is, they only have one clause. We can make much longer and more complex sentences by joining and amalgamating a number of different clauses. For example, the following sentences:

'The girl met the woman.'
'The woman was standing by the canal.'
'They went to a café.'
'They had a meal.'
'They enjoyed it very much.'

can be amalgamated into a multi-clause sentence like this:

'The girl met the woman *who* was standing by the canal *and* they went to a café and had a meal, *which* they enjoyed very much.'

It is possible also to convert some elements of the separate sentences into phrases, e.g. 'The girl met the woman *standing by the canal* ...' etc.

Parts of speech

When considering sentence grammar we need to know various things: What words can be used for subjects? How do we join different sentences? What can come before and after nouns? etc. In other words, we need to be able to talk about *parts of speech*.

The parts of speech which teachers must be able to recognise are summarised in the chart on page 37.

We can now look at each of these parts of speech in more detail.

Noun types

Countable and uncountable: a distinction needs to be made between countable nouns and uncountable nouns. As their name implies, you can 'count' what the words refer to in the first category (and therefore you can make them plural), but you can't count what the words refer to in the second category (and you can't make them plural). A word like 'apple' is countable – we can say 'three apples', 'twenty apples'. So are words like 'table', 'horse', 'cottage' and 'novel'. But words like 'furniture' and 'comfort' are usually uncountable – we can't say '~~two furnitures~~', '~~eight comforts~~'. (See chart on page 38.)

Many words are sometimes countable when they mean one thing but uncountable when they mean something different. For example, the word 'sugar' is uncountable when we say 'I like sugar', 'I'd like some sugar', but countable if we say 'One sugar or two?' (where 'sugar' = spoonful/cube of sugar). When we talk about someone's hair, it is an uncountable noun (we don't say 'He's going bald, he hasn't got ~~many hairs~~' – instead, we say 'He hasn't got much hair'), but we can talk about 'a hair' or 'the hairs on his neck' in which case the word (which has a different meaning) is countable.

Plural nouns, singular verbs: there are some nouns that appear to be plural, but which behave as if they are singular – you can only use them with singular verbs, e.g. 'Darts is a popular pub game', 'The news is depressing'.

part of speech	description	examples (words)	examples (sentences etc.)
noun **(noun phrase)**	a word (or group of words) that is the name of a person, a place, a thing or activity or a quality or idea; nouns can be used as the subject or object of a verb	Eleanor Devon book sense walking stick town hall	Eleanor arrives tomorrow. I love Devon. I recommend this book. Use your common sense. I don't need a walking stick. Meet me at the town hall.
pronoun	a word that is used in place of a noun or noun phrase	her she him they	Jane's husband loves her. She met him two years ago. Look at him! They don't talk much.
adjective	a word that gives more information about a noun or pronoun	kind better impetuous best	What a kind man! We all want a better life! She's so impetuous. That's the best thing about her.
verb	a word (or group of words) which is used in describing an action, experience or state	write ride be set out	He wrote a poem. I like riding horses. We are not amused. She set out on her journey.
adverb **(adverbial phrase)**	a word (or group of words) that describes or adds to the meaning of a verb, adjective, another adverb or a whole sentence	sensibly carefully at home in half an hour	Please talk sensibly. He walked across the bridge carefully. I like listening to music at home. See you in half an hour.
preposition **(prepositional phrase)**	a word (or group of words) which is used to show the way in which other words are connected	for of in on top of	a plan for life Bring me two bottles of wine. Put that in the box. You'll find it on top of the cupboard.
determiner	definite article indefinite article possessives demonstratives quantifiers	the a an my, your etc. this, that, these, those some, many, few etc.	the queen of hearts a princess in love an article in the paper my secret life Look at those photographs! Few people believed him.
conjunction	a word that connects sentences, phrases or clauses	and so but	fish and chips My car broke down, so I went by bus. I like it but I can't afford it.

> EXAMPLES (See Countable and uncountable nouns on page 36.)
> The *weather* is terrible today. (uncountable)
> There isn't much *doubt* about the future. (uncountable)
> He hasn't got much *money*. (uncountable)
> There aren't many *people* out in this storm. (countable)
> She's got a lot of *friends* to help her through this. (countable)
> I've only got a few *coins* in my pocket. (countable)

Collective nouns: nouns which describe groups or organisations (e.g. 'family', 'team', 'government') are called *collective* nouns. They can either be singular or plural depending on whether we are describing the unit or its members. We can say 'The army are advancing' or 'The army is advancing'. This choice isn't usually available in American English, however, where you would expect speakers to use singular verbs only.

Some collective nouns are formed by making adjectives behave like nouns and in this case they are always plural, e.g. 'The poor live in terrible conditions', 'The vertically challenged sometimes feel discriminated against'.

Whether a noun is countable, uncountable, plural or collective affects the construction of the sentences it occurs in. Uncountable nouns are used with singular verbs, and words like 'much'.

Countable nouns, on the other hand, are used with singular or plural verbs and with words like 'many'.

Compound nouns: we are used to nouns being one word. But English also has many compound nouns, constructed from more than one word, e.g. 'walking stick, cherry tree, town hall, boyfriend'.

Not all compound words are nouns, however. We can also have compound adjectives, for example ('fair-skinned, neat-looking').

Noun phrases: some quite long phrases can have the same function in sentences as a single noun. Such phrases, which have a noun at their heart are called *noun phrases*, e.g. 'the man with the hat', 'the tall grinning acrobat', 'the girls I met last night'. In each of these cases the phrase can be the subject or object of a sentence, e.g. '*The man with the hat* ordered a large whisky', 'The children photographed *the tall grinning acrobat*', 'I'm going to ring up *the girls I met last night*'.

Verb types

There are three important types of verb to be aware of: *auxiliary verbs, main verbs* and *phrasal verbs*.

Auxiliary verbs: these are 'be', 'do' and 'have' and the modal auxiliary verbs 'shall', 'should', 'will', 'would', 'can', 'could', 'may', 'might', 'must' or 'ought'. They are used with main verbs (see below) in affirmative sentences, negative sentences and question formation.

> EXAMPLES
> We *are* staying at our friend's house.
> We *have* only just arrived.
> We *don't* expect to stay for long.
> We *can't* afford to pay for a hotel.
> We *ought* to find a place of our own.
> *Could* we move to another town?
> *Did* you live in Glamorgan once?
> We *hadn't* thought of moving.

Note that we often use contractions with auxiliaries, e.g. 'do<u>n't</u>' instead of 'do not', 'we<u>'re</u>' instead of 'we are'.

Main verbs: these carry the main meaning.

> EXAMPLES
> He *arrived* at six o'clock.
> He *said* that he had just *seen* a ghost.
> We didn't *believe* him. He is always *telling* stories.
> He *shouted* at us because we were *laughing* at him.
> Someone *poured* him a drink. He *felt* better after that.

Phrasal verbs: these are formed by adding an adverb or a preposition (or an adverb and a preposition) to a verb to create new meanings, e.g. 'set out' ('We set out the following day' or 'He set out his agenda for the meeting'), which has a completely different meaning from 'set' (e.g. 'set an exam', 'set the table') or 'put up with' ('I'm not going to put up with this any more'), which has a completely different meaning from 'put' (e.g. 'He put her photographs with the letters').

These new two- or three-word verbs are single units of meaning. For example, 'set out' could mean leave on a journey or explain, 'put up with' means tolerate, or stand.

Phrasal verbs confuse students of English because not only do many other languages not have this kind of meaning unit, but also it is difficult to work out when you are dealing with a single unit of meaning (e.g. 'She *looked up* the word in her dictionary') and when you are simply dealing with a verb and a following preposition (e.g. 'She *looked up* at him'.) In the second example, the meaning of 'look' has not been changed by 'up'; in the first it has.

> EXAMPLES
> She *ran over* a dog.
> I'll just *look over* the plans before we start.
> Can we *put off* the wedding till after the funeral?
> I *take after* my father – all his good qualities, that is!
> You won't *get away with* treating her like that.

Verb forms   We describe the *form* of verbs in the following ways.

Present: 'Your brother is upstairs', 'I love it here', 'What's happening?', 'I'm not missing that plane'.

Past: 'Eleanor said goodnight', 'She cried', 'Her parents were packing their suitcases'.

Simple: this is the base form of a verb (e.g. 'walk', 'do', 'run') which can be inflected to agree with the subject ('He walk<u>s</u>', 'She doe<u>s</u>', 'It ru<u>n</u>s') or to indicate time and tense ('They walk<u>ed</u>', 'She d<u>id</u>', 'He r<u>a</u>n as fast as possible').

Continuous: continuous verbs (also called 'progressive') are formed by adding '-ing' to the base form and using it with the verb 'to be,' e.g. 'She is writing a letter', 'She was looking out of the window'.

Present and past verb forms can be described as *present simple*, for example, or *present continuous*, *past simple* or *past continuous*. We can summarise these particular verb forms in the following table.

	simple	**continuous**
present	Mr D'Arcy is in the hall. I love it here.	What's happening? I'm not listening.
past	She said goodbye. She cried. She bought a new phone.	He was waiting at the gate. They were listening to the radio.

Form and meaning: it is tempting to think that when a verb form is called the *present continuous* or the *present simple*, for example, it must always refer to the present. Much of the time this is the case, of course, e.g. 'Look over there! He's sitting in the driver's seat' or 'Gillian has breakfast at seven o'clock every morning', but the verb forms can also have many other uses. In the question, 'What are you doing tomorrow?', the present continuous refers to the future. In storytelling, we often use the present simple to talk about the past, especially to give a sense of drama and immediacy, e.g. 'Last Friday, right? I arrive at the house and knock on the door …'.

What we are saying is that there is no one-to-one correspondence between form and meaning (as we shall see in more detail on page 46). Despite their names, the verb forms mentioned here can be used to talk about different times and different kinds of event or state.

Perfect verbs: perfect verbs are those made with 'have/had' + the past participle or 'have/had been' + the '-ing' form of the verb, e.g. 'I have lived here for six years', 'They had just arrived', 'He's been jogging', 'He hadn't been listening'.

People have struggled for years to explain the meanings of the *present perfect* tense. It has been variously described as suggesting the idea of an action started in the past but continuing up until the present, the idea of an action started in the past which has present relevance, or the idea of an action on a continuum which has not yet finished. Thus, we can say 'I've been to Santiago' and, although we are talking about an event in the past, we don't use the past simple (see above) perhaps because we wish to stress the present relevance of having been to Santiago or because it occurred on the unfinished continuum of 'my life'.

Apart from *present perfect* verb forms with 'have', e.g. 'She's studied Portuguese', we can also have *past perfect* verb forms with 'had', e.g. 'He had been asleep', 'They had been laughing all the way home'. In this case, the verb describes an action before the past and continuing up until that point in the past – or at least having a kind of 'past relevance'.

As with past verb forms, there are both simple and continuous perfect verb forms as the following table shows.

	simple	continuous
present perfect	I have read *Othello*. They haven't arrived yet.	I've been reading *Othello*. They haven't been travelling for long.
past perfect	He had studied English as a child. She hadn't talked to him before.	She'd been living in Argentina for years. They hadn't been talking for more than a minute when ... .

Participles: there are two *participles* in English: *present*, e.g. 'taking', 'talking', 'happening', 'going', and *past*, e.g. 'taken', 'talked', 'happened', 'gone'.

Regular and irregular verbs: we can talk about verbs as *regular* or *irregular*. Regular verbs take the '-ed' ending in the past, e.g. 'talked', 'happened', 'laughed'. Irregular verbs have different past tense forms, e.g. 'ran', 'went', 'bought', 'saw' etc.

Active and passive: another distinction to be made about verbs is that between *active* and *passive*. Active sentences have a subject (S), a verb (V) and an object (O), e.g.

A scene of utter chaos confronted her.
  S   V   O

If we flip things around, however, starting with the object (and in effect making it the subject) we get a passive sentence, e.g.

She was confronted by a scene of utter chaos.

Passives are formed by the auxiliary + past participle of the verb in question. The past participles in the following chart are in *italics*.

tenses	examples
present simple continuous	It's *made* in Taiwan. They're being *processed* right now.
past simple continuous	He was *met* by the President. The plan was being *discussed*.
present perfect past perfect	She's been *photographed* many times. They had been *seen* in the area.
future with 'will'	You'll be *taken* to the airport by taxi.
future perfect	The job will have been *completed* by then.
'going to'	They're going to be *offered* a new holiday.

Passive constructions are often used when we don't know or want to say who did something (e.g. 'It's been destroyed', 'It was decided that you should leave') or when we want to give a different emphasis to the subject and object of an action.

Verb complementation: this describes what words and kinds of words we can use after particular verbs. As we saw with modal auxiliaries, some verbs are followed by infinitives ('I can *swim*', 'He should *go*'), some are followed by 'to' + infinitive ('I like *to swim*', 'He tried *to save* her'), some are followed by participles ('I don't enjoy *running*'), and some by 'that' + a new clause. There are many other complementation patterns too. Some verbs can be followed by more than one grammatical pattern.

EXAMPLES
I like *to watch* TV / I like *watching* TV.
I must *go*. (not I ~~must to go~~.)
I explained *the problem to him*. (not I ~~explained him the problem~~.)
She protected *me from the dragon*. (not she ~~protected me to the dragon~~.)
She suggested *that I trained* as a teacher. (not she ~~suggested me to train as a teacher~~.)

Pronouns

Types of pronoun: there are three basic types of pronoun: *personal pronouns*, *reflexive* (personal) *pronouns* and *relative pronouns*.

Personal pronouns: personal pronouns are 'I', 'you', 'he', 'she', 'we' and 'they'

– and 'it' which isn't really personal at all! Not only do they have these subject realisations, however, but they can be object pronouns ('I saw *him*'), reflexive pronouns ('I cut *myself*'), and possessive pronouns ('Give it to me. It's *mine!*'). We can summarise personal pronouns in the following chart.

subject	object	reflexives	possessives
I	me	myself	mine
you	you	yourself	yours
he	him	himself	his
she	her	herself	hers
it	it	itself	its
we	us	ourselves	ours
you	you	yourselves	yours
they	them	themselves	theirs

Relative pronouns: the pronouns 'who', 'whose', 'where', 'which' and 'that' are used to join clauses/ideas. If we have the following two ideas (1) 'I saw a girl', (2) 'she was wearing a beautiful blue dress', we can stick them together with a relative pronoun, e.g. 'I saw a girl *who* was wearing a beautiful blue dress'. We call 'who was wearing a beautiful blue dress' a relative clause.

EXAMPLES
The man *who* walked into my office was tall and blond.
She gave me a pen *that* I still use.
That's the school *where* I taught my first class.
That's the woman *whose* courage saved her child.
The saxophone is the instrument *which* makes the nicest sound.

Adjectives

Adjectives can be used before and after nouns. They can have many forms.

Comparative and superlative: adjectives can be made *comparative* ('good → better', 'nice → nicer', 'young → younger') and *superlative* ('best', 'nicest', 'youngest'). They fall into a number of categories: one-syllable adjectives generally add '-er' or '-est' to become comparative and superlative; some adjectives are *irregular*, like 'good', 'bad' etc.; adjectives which end in vowel + consonant double the final consonant, like 'big → bigger', 'thin → thinner' etc.; and adjectives that end in 'y' usually change the 'y' to 'i' like 'silly → sillier', 'friendly → friendlier'.

Longer adjectives – three or more syllables – stay the same and are prefaced by 'more' or 'most'. The same is true of some two-syllable adjectives ('more careful', 'most pleasant') while others like 'clever' can be both 'cleverer' and 'more clever' in modern English usage.

adjective	comparative	superlative
good	better	best
big	bigger	biggest
nice	nicer	nicest
young	younger	youngest
silly	sillier	silliest
clever	cleverer/more clever	cleverest/most clever
interesting	more interesting	more interesting

Adjective order: When we use a string of adjectives, there is a generally accepted order.

$$size \rightarrow colour \rightarrow origin \rightarrow material \rightarrow purpose \rightarrow noun$$

		size	colour	origin	material	purpose	noun
e.g.	the	small	purple	German	silk	evening	gown
	the	large	( )	( )	wooden	( )	crate

Adjective and preposition: many adjectives are followed by specific prepositions, e.g. 'interested in', 'keen on', 'happy about' etc.

Adjectives as nouns: we can use some adjectives as if they were nouns, e.g. 'the blind', 'the poor' etc.

Adverbs

Adverbs and adverbial phrases can be of *time* ('early', 'late', 'yesterday morning'), *manner* ('He played *well*', 'She ran *quickly*', 'He spoke *fiercely*') and *place* ('They work *upstairs*', 'I live *in Cambridge*', 'You'll burn *in hell* for this').

Adverb position: adverbs usually appear at the end of sentences, but they can sometimes be used at the beginning or in the middle.

Most adverbs of frequency ('always', 'usually', 'often', 'sometimes' etc.) can usually go at the beginning, middle or end of a sentence, e.g. '*Sometimes* he rings me up in the morning', 'He *sometimes* rings me up in the morning', 'He rings me up in the morning *sometimes*'. But this often depends on the particular adverb being used (for example 'never' can only occur in the middle position).

Adverbs cannot usually come between a verb and its object. We say 'I usually have sandwiches for lunch' but not 'I have usually sandwiches for lunch'.

Modifying adverbs: adverbs can modify adjectives, e.g. 'a *wonderfully* physical performance', 'an *unusually* large cucumber', 'a *really* fascinating film' etc.

Prepositions

Position of prepositions: prepositions ('at', 'in', 'on', 'for', 'of', 'with' etc.) usually come before a noun but can also come at the end of a clause with certain structures. For example, we can say 'The book's *on* the shelf' or 'It's not something I'm very interested *in*'.

Particular prepositions: many words and expressions can only be followed by particular prepositions, e.g. 'anxious about', 'dream about/of', 'good at', 'kind to' etc.

Prepositions and adverbs: some words can be both prepositions and also adverbs (often called adverbial particles). In the sentence 'She climbed down the ladder', 'down' is a preposition because it has an object ('the ladder'). In 'She sat down', it is an adverb because it does not have an object.

Articles

Determiners: articles ('the', 'a', 'an') belong to a class of words called *determiners*. Other examples of determiners are 'this', 'that', 'these',' those', 'some', 'all of'. Determiners usually come before a noun or at the beginning of a noun phrase, e.g. '*an* apple', '*the* red bus', '*some* of my best friends', '*a* Spanish teacher I know'.

Definite article: we use the *definite article* ('the') when we think that the reader or listener knows which particular thing or person we are talking about or when there can only be one, e.g. '*the* Pope' (we know which one because there is only one), '*the* book I read' (= we both know which one I'm talking about), '*the* oldest man in the world' (because there can only be one 'oldest' man) etc.

We do not use the definite article when we are talking about people and things in general using plural or uncountable nouns, e.g. 'Teachers should establish a good rapport with their students', 'Life's a beach' (a Californian saying), 'People who live in glass houses should buy curtains' etc.

However, just to confuse things, we do sometimes make general statements with the definite article and a singular noun, e.g. '*The* great white shark is a dangerous creature in the wrong situation' (see also the indefinite article below).

Indefinite article: the *indefinite article* ('a/an') is used to refer to a particular person or thing when the listener/reader doesn't know which one is being described, e.g. '*A* man was reading the paper', 'I saw *a* plane take off', 'I'm going to buy *a* new computer'.

As with the definite article (see above), we can also use 'a/an' to refer to a member of a group – in order to refer to the whole group, e.g. '*A* man's gotta do what a man's gotta do', '*A* good nurse will always spend time with his patients' etc.

Conjunctions and conditionals

Conjunctions: these join two clauses, e.g. 'Nicky said goodnight *and* walked out of the house with a heavy heart', 'She was going to be away for a fortnight *so* she took a large suitcase', 'I can sing *but* I can't play the guitar', 'I'm a teacher *because* I like working with people' etc.

We only use one conjunction for two clauses. We say 'Although it was early he jumped out of bed', not ~~'Although it was early but he jumped out of bed'~~.

Conditional sentences: these are formed when the conjunction 'if' is used to preface a condition, e.g. '*If* it rains (*condition*), you'll get wet (*result*)'. In this case, it is quite likely that it will rain, and therefore the result is possible. However, if we change the sentence to '*If* it rained, you would get wet' we are suggesting that the chance of it raining is unlikely – in other words, we are talking *hypothetically* – and this is signalled by the use of 'would' rather than 'will'. A further change of verb tense/form (using the past perfect) will produce an impossible condition, e.g. '*If* it had rained, you would have got wet'. But it didn't so you were spared!

These three conditional forms are often called *first*, *second* and *third* conditionals. It is useful to understand whether they are *real* (= possible/likely) or *hypothetical* (= unlikely/impossible) and whether they refer to the present, future or past. The following table gives some examples of this.

	real	**hypothetical**
talking about the present	If you pay by cash, you get a discount.	If I had a dog, I'd take it for walks.
talking about the future	If you work hard, you'll pass the exam.	If I won the lottery, I'd travel around the world. If I were you, I'd get a new jacket.
talking about the past	If it was very warm, we ate outside.	If I'd known about the rail strike, I would have come by car.

However, it is important to realise that there are many conditional clauses which fall outside these basic patterns by using a variety of different tenses and verb types, e.g. 'If you finish before time, hand your papers in and go', 'If I'd been informed about this, I could solve the problem' – and, in American English, 'If I would have met her earlier, I would have married her', though this use of 'would' in both clauses (instead of only in the *result* clause) is considered unacceptable by many speakers of British English.

Forms and meanings

One form, many meanings: on page 40 we saw how the present continuous can refer to both the present ('I'm not listening') and the future ('I'm seeing him tomorrow'). It can be used to refer to a temporary uncompleted event ('They are enjoying the weather') or to a series of completed events ('He's always putting his foot in it'). What is happening is that the same basic form (the present continuous) is being used to express a number of different concepts of time and duration.

Individual words can mean more than one thing too, for example, 'book'

(= something to read, to reserve, a list of bets etc), 'beat' (= to win, to hit, to mix (an egg), the 'pulse' (of music/a heart)) and 'can' (= ability, permission, probability – and a container made of aluminium). Notice that, in these examples, not only can the same form have many meanings, but it can also be different parts of speech.

With so many available meanings for words and grammatical forms, it is the context the word occurs in which determines which of these meanings is being referred to. If we say 'I beat him because I ran faster than he did', 'beat' is likely to mean win rather than physically assault or mix (though there is always the possibility of ambiguity, of course). Likewise, the present continuous changes its meaning with different time adverbials. The sentence 'I'm talking to the president' changes dramatically if we use these different expressions: 'at this very minute' or 'tomorrow at noon'.

One meaning, many forms: one form can have many meanings, therefore, but it is also true that a meaning or concept can be expressed in many different ways. Consider, for example, the concept of 'the future'. We have already seen the present continuous used for this, but we can also use different forms to express the same basic concept.

EXAMPLES
I'll see you tomorrow.
I'm going to win the race – with luck.
I can get to you by tomorrow evening.
The president arrives at her home on Saturday.

However, it is worth pointing out that each different form has a slightly different meaning – even if they are all 'future' sentences.

The same is true of word meaning. Even where words appear to have the same meaning – to be synonyms, in other words – they are usually distinct from each other. For example, we can describe an intelligent person with a number of different words: 'intelligent', 'bright', 'brainy', 'clever', 'smart' etc. But each of these words has a different connotation. 'Brainy' is an informal word and might well have a negative connotation when used by a schoolchild about her colleague. 'Bright' carries the connotation of lively, young. 'Smart' is commonly used in American English and has a slightly tricky connotation. 'Clever' is often used in phrases with negative connotations, e.g. 'too clever by half', 'He may be clever but he's not going to get away with it'.

What is clear is that students and teachers need to be aware of the fact that form does not equal meaning and vice-versa. Even where two different forms appear to have the same meaning, you will usually find a difference in those meanings somewhere.

Language functions

An exasperated teacher tells a habitually late student 'You'd better get here on time next class!' She is making a recommendation, something which is between advice and an order.

There are other ways in which the teacher can make recommendations, too.

> EXAMPLES
>
> I suggest you get here on time next class.
>
> I'd get here on time next class if I was/were you.
>
> I strongly recommend that you get here on time next class.
>
> I think it would be a really good idea if you got here on time next class.

As we can see, the *function* of making a recommendation can be realised in a number of different ways (much in the same way that we can express the future in a number of separate grammatical realisations).

A language function is a purpose you wish to achieve when you say or write something. By 'performing' the function you are performing an act of communication. If you say 'I invite you' you are performing the function of inviting, if you say 'I apologise', you are performing the function of apologising. Of course, you could also say 'D'you want to come to the cinema?' to invite someone or 'Sorry' to apologise.

As with our example suggestions above, there are, of course, many different ways/forms of *inviting, apologising, agreeing, giving advice, asking for information* etc.

If our students want to express themselves in speaking or writing, they need to know how to perform these functions – in other words how to use grammar and vocabulary to express certain meanings/purposes.

Words together: collocation

Before leaving the subject of meaning, we will look at a particular feature of vocabulary use which language speakers need to know about, whether consciously or subconsciously.

'How was your lesson?' a teacher asks a colleague. 'A complete disaster!' he replies. 'Complete' is a word which quite often co-occurs (collocates) with the word 'disaster'. He could also have said 'total disaster' and, perhaps, 'utter disaster'. However, he would not say 'full disaster' or 'whole disaster' even though his meaning would be clear.

What we find is that some words live happily together and other words don't. There are collocations which work and collocations which don't. We talk about 'common/good sense', but not 'bad sense', 'making the bed' but not 'making the housework' (in the last, we use 'doing the housework'), we can say 'harmful/damaging effects', but not 'bad effects' etc.

Speaking and writing

A typical piece of informal spoken English looks something like this.

A: Hi.
B: Hi.
A: Come in.
B: Thanks.
A: Cup of coffee?
B: Great.
A: Come on through.
B: Cold!
A: Yes, cold. Really cold. I nearly froze out there earlier this morning. Here's your coffee.
B: Thanks. That's better. How've you spent your day?
A: Reading a magazine.
B: Anything interesting?

Characteristics of speech: we immediately notice some characteristics of spoken English in this extract. Firstly, people speak in incomplete sentences, e.g. 'Cold' instead of 'It's cold', 'Cup of coffee?' instead of 'Would you like a cup of coffee?', 'Anything interesting?' instead of 'Was there anything interesting in it?'. Secondly, speakers repeat what each other says (and themselves), e.g. 'Cold!' 'Yes, cold, really cold.' Speakers also tend to use contractions ('here's', 'that's', 'how've') whereas in writing we usually use the full form of the auxiliary verbs ('here is', 'that is', 'how have').

Recent research has also shown that different words are used differently in speech and writing. 'However' is more common in writing than speaking, for example, but 'started' is much more common than 'began' in speaking. People use 'go' to mean 'said' ('She goes how you feeling and I go not so bad ...') in speech but almost never in writing.

Paralinguistic features: there are many non-linguistic ways in which speech can be affected. Speakers can change the tone of their voices and the emphasis they give. They can speak faster or slower, louder or softer. And if they are involved in face-to-face communication they can use their expressions and body language too.

Writing devices: writing has its own set of tricks:
   − dashes
   ! exclamations marks
   new paragraphs
   , commas
   CAPITAL letters etc.
All of these can be used to create rhythm and effect. But whereas i the participants can clarify what they are saying as thev depending on who they are talking to, in writing it's much m⌐ to get it absolutely right. Writing tends to be more precise devices to keep it going − as we shall see in Chapter 8.

Pronunciation

There are three areas we need to know about in the pronunciation of English – apart from speed and volume – which are intimately connected with meaning.

Sounds: words are made up of individual sounds (or phonemes). For example 'beat' = /b + iː + t/ (iː is the symbol for the sound 'ee'), 'coffee' = /ˈkɒfiː/ and 'cease' = /siːs/.

Sounds (phonemes) are represented here by phonetic symbols (/b/, /iː/ and /k/ for example). This is because there is no one–to–one correspondence between written letters and spoken sounds. Thus the 'c' of 'cat' is pronounced differently from the 'c' of 'cease', but is the same as the 'c' of 'coffee'. 'Though', 'trough', and 'rough' all have the '-ou-' spelling but it is pronounced differently in each case. Different spellings can have the same sound too: 'plane' and 'gain' both have the same vowel sound, but they are spelt differently.

By changing one sound, we can change the word and its meaning. If we replace the sound /b/ with the sound /m/, for example we get 'meat' instead of 'beat'. And if we change /iː/ to /ɪ/ we get 'bit' instead of 'beat'. A complete list of phonetic symbols is given in Appendix C on page 191.

Stress: the second area of importance is stress – in other words, where emphasis is placed in words and sentences.

The *stressed syllable* (the syllable which carries the main stress) is that part of a word or phrase which has the greatest emphasis because the speaker increases the volume or changes the pitch of their voice when saying that syllable, e.g. 'imp<u>or</u>tant', 'comp<u>lain</u>', '<u>me</u>dicine' etc. And in many longer words, there is both a *main* stress and a *secondary* stress, e.g. int<u>er</u>pret<u>a</u>tion, where 'ter' has the secondary stress and 'ta' the main stress. In addition, different varieties of English can often stress words differently. For example, British English speakers usually say 'ad<u>ver</u>tisement' whereas some American speakers say 'advert<u>ise</u>ment'. The placing of stress can also affect the meaning of a word. For example, '<u>im</u>port' is a noun, but 'imp<u>ort</u>' is a verb.

In phrases and sentences, we give special emphasis to certain parts of the sentence (by changing our pitch, increasing the volume etc), e.g. 'I'm a teacher because I like <u>people</u>'. But we could change the meaning of the sentence by placing the stress somewhere else, for example, 'I'm a teacher because I <u>like</u> people'. You can imagine this being said as an angry response to someone asking a teacher to do something terrible to their students. If, on the other hand, the sentence is said with the main stress on the word 'I' it is suggested that this is what makes the speaker different from others who do not like people.

Teachers use a variety of symbols to show stress, e.g.

'teacher   performance   rap<u>port</u>   engagement

Pitch and intonation: *pitch* describes the level at which you speak. Some people have high-pitched voices, others say things in a low-pitched voice.

When we pitch the words we say, we may use a variety of different levels: higher when we are excited or terrified, for example, but lower when we are sleepy or bored. *Intonation* is often described as the music of speech. It encompasses the moments at which we change the pitch of our voices in order to give certain messages. It is absolutely crucial for getting our meaning across. The word 'Yes', for example, can be said with a falling voice, a rising voice or a combination of the two. By changing the direction of the voice we can make 'Yes' mean 'I agree' or 'Perhaps it's true' or 'You can't be serious' or 'Wow, you are so right' or any number of other things.

Teachers often use arrows or wavy lines to show intonation tunes (pitch change), like this:

You're not angry, are you?   or   You do love me, don't you?

Notice that the first question seems to be a genuine request for information, whereas the second is asking for confirmation of something the speaker assumes to be true. We know this because the two different intonations convey two different meanings.

Conclusions

In this chapter we have
- made it clear that this short chapter is only the briefest introduction to a huge subject and suggested that it should be read in conjunction with the Task File on pages 148–152.
- studied sentence construction, showing how sentences are constructed of and from subjects, verbs, objects, complements and adverbials.
- looked at aspects of nouns, verbs, adjectives, adverbs, prepositions, determiners and conjunctions.
- noticed that a grammatical form or a word doesn't guarantee its meaning. Words and structures can have many meanings just as similar concepts can be represented by different forms or words.
- examined the differences between speech and writing. Each has its different characteristics and students need to know about these. As teachers, part of our job is to expose students to written and (spontaneous) spoken English.
- looked at three aspects of pronunciation: sounds, stress and intonation.

Looking ahead

- In the next chapter we are going to look at how to study language – including grammatical patterns, pronunciation, word formation and word meaning.
- In the chapters on reading and writing (7 and 8) we will pay attention to the special features of writing we have discussed in this chapter.
- In the chapter on listening (10) we will look at taped examples of spontaneous speech and talk about how students can be helped to deal with them.

How to teach language

- What does language study consist of?
- How should we expose students to language?
- How can we help students to understand meaning?
- How can we help students to understand language form?
- How should students practise language?
- Why do students make mistakes?
- How should teachers correct students?
- Where do language study activities fit in teaching sequences?

What does language study consist of?

Whatever the level of the students and however language *Study* is organised within *ESA* teaching sequences, there are four things that students need to do with 'new' language: be exposed to it, understand its meaning, understand its form (how it is constructed) and practise it.

In the sections that follow, we will analyse each of these issues in some detail in the light of the study of the following areas of language: the verb 'to be' + noun (e.g. 'It's a pen'), simple invitations, the use of comparative adjectives, and the word 'protection'.

To get an overall idea of the teaching procedures envisaged for each language point, readers can turn to page 64 where we show how *Study* fits into teaching sequences. Before that, however, we will look at the four *Study* issues (listed above) in detail, giving examples in each case for the language points being discussed.

How should we expose students to language?

In a classroom, a major part of the teacher's job is to expose students to language so that they can use it later. Here are some examples of how we can do this.

Example 1: 'It's a pen' (complete beginners)

The teacher is with a group of complete beginners. She wants them to be able to say what objects are called. She holds up a pen, points to it and says 'pen ... look ... pen ... pen' as many times as she thinks it is necessary. The students have had a chance to hear the word.

Later, she may want to go beyond single words. She can hold up the pen and say 'Listen ... it's a pen ... it's a pen ... it's a pen'. Once again, she is giving students a chance to hear the sound of the new language before they try to use it themselves. Later still, she may start asking the question 'What is it? (*pointing to the pen*) ... What is it?' so that students get a chance to hear what the question sounds like.

Because many people acquire languages by hearing them first, many teachers prefer to expose students to the spoken form first (as in this example). However, some students may need the reassurance of the written word as well.

Example 2: invitations (elementary)

The teacher wants her elementary students to be able to invite each other and respond to invitations. She plays a tape on which the following dialogue is heard.

SARAH: Joe! Hello.
JOE: Oh hello, Sarah.
SARAH: Umm. How are you?
JOE: Fine. Why?
SARAH: Er ... no reason ... (*pause ... nervously*) Are you doing anything this evening?
JOE: No. Why?
SARAH: Would you like to come to the cinema?
JOE: Yes, that would be great. Well, it depends. What's on?
SARAH: The new Tarantino film.
JOE: I suppose it's all violent.
SARAH: Yeah. Probably. But it's meant to be really good.
JOE: I don't usually like violent films.
SARAH: Oh. OK. Well, we could go to the pizza place or something.
JOE: I'm only joking! I'd love to come.

The teacher plays the tape more than once so that students get a good chance to hear the invitation language – some of which (the present continuous, vocabulary items) they probably already know. She may also say the invitation part of the dialogue herself and she may feel it is a good idea to show the students a written version.

Example 3: comparatives (lower intermediate)

In this example for lower intermediate students, the teacher is going to get students to use comparative adjectives. Before she does this, however, she has them read the text opposite.

FEAR OF FLYING

How can anyone like flying? It's a crazy thing to do. Birds fly; people don't. I hate flying. You wait for hours for the plane to take off, and it's often late. The plane's always crowded. You can't walk around and there's nothing to do. You can't open the windows and you can't get off. The seats are uncomfortable, there's no choice of food and there are never enough toilets. Then after the plane lands, it's even worse. It takes hours to get out of the airport and into the city.

I prefer travelling by train. Trains are much better than planes; they're cheaper, safer, and more comfortable. You can walk around in a train and open the windows. Stations are more convenient than airports, because you can get on and off in the middle of cities. If you miss a train, you can always catch another one later. Yes, trains are slower, but speed isn't everything. Staying alive and enjoying yourself is more important!

From *Look Ahead 2* by
Andy Hopkins and Jocelyn Potter

This text gives students many examples of comparative adjectives used in a fairly realistic way.

Example 4: 'protection' (upper intermediate)

With an upper intermediate class, the teacher wants the students to be able to use the word 'protection' correctly. She shows them the following printout from a computer.

I was married, pregnant; and had a dog for protection. 'I dream of your body so luscious an SPF rating. Now, generally, SPF 2 is low on protection, but Bergasol's skin type 2 is high get wet! These sunscreens do give the best protection - after all perspiration can wash sunscreen after swimming. Use a higher sun protection factor (SPF) on vulnerable spots exhibited a wide variation in the effective protection accorded to the import-substitute negligence in not providing adequate police protection for the city. Several weeks free needles will provide any significant protection. A sufferer from drug addiction Annual 'boosters'... provide inexpensive protection for your dog against... diseases was of comparable importance. For the farmer protection against a severe decline in his her belly. This meagre shelter gives little protection from either enemies or the wind also responded to the desire of business for protection against foreign competition. The jugglers who require an excess of praise and protection from hard truths. sprays. Your medication may not give absolute protection against malaria, some forms of Whereat she shrieked and turned to Summers for protection. He assured her she need fear that citizens might value. Integrity provides protection against partiality or deceit or everything. There was a mask, a visor for eye protection. If it was hot outside it was even to hasten its recovery, began to give it protection against the import of foreign foods stems from any inadequacies of employment protection legislation. The employment of the villagers but with clothing, food, and protection against the sun. But his feelings of their people and for their defence – and protection of the environment and the worker to fall again. My sealskin coat was a good protection against the wind and my hands were if Mother approves and continues to offer protection. The ogre's wife hides Jack in a to their ancestors for life and health, and for protection against their enemies. When they a diversified line. This provides further protection. There is danger that technological scrutiny, the bureaucratic system can provide protection against allegations of corruption industry in the country was given increased protection. This was simply the first dose of can't promise you total and utter and complete protection. All I can promise is that we can only in terms of the general need for consumer protection, which is encompassed in new clause who have a good record in environmental protection are officially commended and

Edited sample from the *Longman-Lancaster Corpus*

It shows many examples of the word (in the centre) being used. The examples are taken from a wide variety of sources (books, newspapers, advertisements etc.) which have been fed into a computer. Any word can be looked up in the same way to see how and when it is used. The number of words to the right and left of the search word (the word in the centre) is just enough for us to understand the word's meaning and use correctly in each case.

How can we help students to understand meaning?

Some of the ways we can help students to understand the meaning of new language are illustrated in the following examples.

Example 1: 'It's a pen' (complete beginners)

This is perhaps the easiest level at which to explain meaning. The teacher wants the students to understand the meaning of the form 'pen' so she holds up a pen and says 'pen'. The meaning will be clear. She can do the same with words like 'pencil', 'table', 'chair' etc.

When, however, she wants to expose students to the question form 'What is it?' she cannot rely on objects. Instead, she asks the question using gestures (raised shoulders and open arms) and expressions (a puzzled look on her face) to indicate the meaning of the question.

Of course, the teacher can also ensure that students understand the meaning of a word by showing pictures (photographs, cards etc.) or by drawing them on the board (even 'amateur' stick drawings are useful for this purpose).

Some of the ways of helping students to understand, then – especially when dealing with fairly simple concepts – are: objects, pictures, drawings, gesture and expression.

Example 2: invitations (elementary)

In this example, the teacher starts by showing the students a picture of Sarah and Joe. She gets the students to ask their names and tells them what the names are. Then she asks them to speculate on what their relationship is ('Do you think they are friends?') to establish the fact that Sarah likes Joe.

After she has played the tape of the invitation dialogue she can ask them questions to check they have understood the situation, for example:

'What does Sarah want?'
'What language does she use?'
'Does Joe accept?'
'What are they going to do?' etc.

The use of questions like these (often called check questions) establishes that students have understood what the language means.

The teacher could also draw a picture of Sarah with a 'think' bubble coming out of her head which says 'me -> cinema + Joe??!!'

Example 3: comparatives (lower intermediate)

In the 'Fear of Flying' text, the teacher can start by asking 'How does the writer prefer travelling?' She can then explain the meaning of individual adjectives. She could show a picture of a beautiful sofa and say 'comfortable' and follow it with a picture of an old school chair and say 'not comfortable'. She could then show a picture of a nice armchair followed by the really comfortable sofa and say 'The armchair is comfortable but the sofa is more comfortable than the armchair'. She could use check questions to see if the students have understood the other comparative concepts, e.g. 'Which is safer, mountain climbing or watching television?' or 'Which is slower, walking or running?'

Anything which helps students understand meaning is worth trying. For example, some teachers like to use time lines to explain tenses. The following attempts to show the meaning of 'I've been living here since 1992' in graphic form.

1992   Now

A time line

Example 4: 'protection' (upper intermediate)

The teacher may not need to explain the meaning of 'protection' to the students since they can either work it out for themselves (by looking at the computer printout) or check in a dictionary.

Explaining the meaning of abstract concepts is often difficult and time-consuming but it may need to be done. We can explain the meaning of 'vegetable' by listing different kinds of vegetable, we can explain the meaning of 'hot' through mime (burning ourselves) or by explaining what it is the opposite of. 'Sad' and 'happy' can be explained by expression, pictures, music etc. But words like 'protection' or 'charity' are more difficult!

One way of doing it is to show them enough examples of the word being used so that its meaning emerges naturally (that's what computer concordances do – e.g. page 54). Another possibility is to ask students to write their own dictionary definitions and then check them with a good learners' dictionary. The teacher could ask them to explain what the word means or – in the case of 'protection' – she can simply explain that the word means 'safety from danger/discomfort' etc.

How can we help students to understand language form?

As well as hearing/seeing language – and understanding what it means – students need to know how it is constructed, how the bits fit together. Whether the teacher gives them this information or whether they work it out for themselves, they need to comprehend the constituent sounds, syllables, words and phrases of the new language as the following examples show.

Example 1: 'It's a pen' (complete beginners)

When the teacher first says 'pen' she can then show what the sounds in the word are by saying them one by one, e.g. 'pen ... pen ..: /p/ ... /e/ ... /n/ ... pen ...'. By picking out the bits in this way, she clearly explains the sound construction of the word.

Some sounds can be demonstrated. The sound /p/ for example is made by forcing the lips apart with air from the lungs: the teacher can point to her mouth and show this happening. However, some sounds which are created at the back of the mouth (like /g/ and /k/) are more difficult to demonstrate in this way.

When the teacher introduces words of more than one syllable she will want to make sure that the students know which syllable is stressed. So, when she says 'table', she may exaggerate the 'ta' syllable and add even more emphasis by clicking her fingers or stamping her foot on the stressed syllable. When she writes the word on the board, she will indicate which syllable is stressed in one of the ways we looked at on page 50.

The exaggerated use of voice and gesture are also important for demonstrating intonation. When the teacher wants to demonstrate the question 'What is it?' she can make the voice fall dramatically on 'is' before rising slightly on 'it' and she can accompany this by making falling (and rising) gestures with her arm very much like the conductor of an orchestra.

The bits that make up the phrase 'It's a pen' need to be clear in the students' minds too. One way of doing this is for the teacher to say the bits one by one (just like the sounds, e.g. 'It is a pen ... it ... is ... a ... pen ... it ... is ....a ... pen ... it's a pen') or she can write the following on the board.

It	is	a	pen. table. computer.

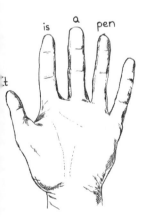

A particular feature of spoken and informal written English is the way in which we contract auxiliary verb forms. We tend to say 'It's a pen' not 'It is a pen'; we say 'I'll see you tomorrow' not 'I will see you tomorrow'. This can easily be demonstrated with hand movements and gestures etc. For example, if the teacher makes her two hands into loose fists and shows that one represents 'it' and the other represents 'is' she can then bring them together to give a clear visual demonstration of 'it's'. A similar technique which has been very popular is to use fingers. The teacher points to each of her fingers in turn, giving each finger a word, as in this illustration.

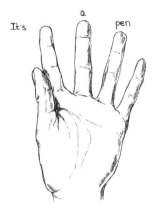

It's   a   pen

Then she lets students see her bring two fingers together to show the contraction, as in this illustration.

Some teachers use small wooden blocks of different lengths and colours (called Cuisenaire rods) to show word and sentence stress and construction and there are other visual possibilities too: cards, drawings, getting students to physically stand in line as if they were word and sentence elements.

The point of all these techniques is to demonstrate to students how the elements of language add up. So the trick, for the teacher, is to work out what the important features of a word, phrase or grammatical structure are and how the bits fit together.

Example 2: invitations (elementary)

With language like invitations, it may be helpful to treat some consecutive words of the invitation as a single unit. In other words, we can take more than one word and treat them as one chunk of meaning, e.g.

'Would you like to' + verb phrase etc.
'That would be' + adjective

The teacher can then ask students for alternatives for 'come to the cinema?', e.g. 'come to the party/theatre', 'have lunch/have a drink'. She can pretend to have one phrase in her left hand 'would you like to' and another in the right 'come to the cinema' and then draw them together. Or she can write the following on the board.

Would you like to	come to the party? come to the theatre? have lunch? have a drink?

As with our previous example, the teacher will say the question 'Would you like to come to the cinema?' and the answer 'That would be great' with exaggerated stress and intonation using gesture and expression to help students understand what the language sounds like.

Example 3: comparatives (lower intermediate)

In the book from which the 'Fear of Flying' text was taken, the students are given the exercise on the next page.

Look back at the article and answer the questions.

1 What is the comparative form of these adjectives?
safe – *safer*
safe comfortable convenient cheap slow important good bad
2 What rules can you make about the comparative form of:
a) most short adjectives?
b) long adjectives?
Are there any irregular adjectives which do not fit these rules?

When the teacher asks students to do this exercise she is asking them to discover the construction (of comparative adjectives) for themselves. Both she and the textbook writers think that the students will be able to work it out without having to be told – and that this 'discovery' will be more memorable for them than if she simply tells them.

Of course, there's no reason why a book is needed for discovery activities. Teachers can always ask students to work things out by using their own questions and procedures. What is important is that the teacher should be there to tell them if they have worked out the rules correctly.

The teacher will want to make sure that the students know what a comparative sentence sounds like. She can say 'Trains are cheaper than planes' showing through voice and gesture how the rhythm and stress of the sentence works.

Example 4: 'protection' (upper intermediate)

Students clearly need to know how 'protection' is spelt and what it sounds like – it is stressed on the second syllable etc. But the computer printout tells us more than that, and the teacher can help students to see what is there.

She can start by asking the simple question 'What comes before and after the word "protection"?' and students working together or individually will be able to provide the following answers.

A common pattern into which 'protection' fits is '... protection against + article + noun' but as the printout shows we can also say '... protection for/from...'.

The verbs which come before 'protection' in our sample include 'provide', 'offer' and 'give'.

Adjectives which commonly come immediately before 'protection' include 'effective', 'complete' and 'environmental'.

As a result of this we can ask students to provide their own table showing where 'protection' fits, for example:

offer provide give	effective environmental complete	protection	against from for

Or we can encourage students to write 'protection' in their own personal vocabulary books giving the same kind of information, e.g.

protection – offer/provide/give protection against/from/for

Of course, this information is available in good dictionaries, but it is not so memorable, perhaps, when referred to there. Because the students have studied the computer printout themselves – and worked out and discovered facts about the word 'protection' on their own – their understanding of the construction of the word and its grammatical surroundings is likely to be much greater and more profound.

How should students practise language?

If and when students have been exposed to language whose meaning and construction they understand, it makes sense for them to practise it under controlled conditions. This will allow them to check that they have got it right.

Practice should not go on for too long, however. There are many other things that teachers and students want to do in classrooms and too much practice will take time away from them.

Example 1: 'It's a pen' (complete beginners)

Repetition can be very useful for students especially at beginner level. It gives them a chance to see if they've understood what's happened so far and if they have, it gives them the confidence to try and use the language themselves.

The simplest kind of repetition is for the teacher to say 'pen ... pen' and then get students to say 'pen' altogether, in chorus. This can be good fun and allows students to try the new word out with everybody else rather than having to risk getting it wrong in front of the class.

After choral repetition, the teacher can ask students to repeat the word individually (now that they've had a chance to say it in safety). She calls them by name or points to them or indicates who should speak in some other way and they say the word. She then corrects them if they are not getting it quite right (as we shall see on page 63).

Choral and individual repetition are useful for sentences as well as words. The teacher may well use both techniques for sentences like 'It's a pen' and 'What is it?'

It is, however, important to move beyond simple repetition during practice. We want students to be able to use a combination of the new grammar with the vocabulary items they have learnt so the teacher gets students to make similar sentences by prompting them with different words, objects or pictures. She may hold up a pen and indicate a student so that the student will say 'It's a pen'. Then she holds up a pencil and indicates another student so that they will say 'It's a pencil'. She can point to the table for the sentence 'It's a table' and so on.

Practice sessions at this level are likely to be a combination of repetition and simple sentence-making of the kind the teacher is using in this example. With different words and constructions, she may not be able to hold up objects or point to them; instead she can use pictures, drawings, mime, gesture, words etc.

Example 2: invitations (elementary)

As with the previous example, the teacher can get choral and individual repetition of the key phrases 'Would you like to come to the cinema?' and 'That would be great'. When she has done that, she can get one student to ask the question and another student to answer.

Now she can ask students to make different invitations. She can try and elicit alternatives. She can then prompt them by saying 'concert' for them to say 'Would you like to come to the concert?' and 'nice' for 'That would be nice'. She may also want to give them the option of 'I'm afraid I can't' or 'No, thank you'.

If she thinks students need more opportunity to practise this question-and-answer exchange, she can put them in pairs to make as many invitations and replies as they can. While they are doing this, she can go round listening and helping where necessary – or she can stand at the front of the class getting an idea of how it is going before stopping the pairs and hearing one or two of them with the whole class.

In very large classes, it may be useful to divide the class in half: one half is Sarah, the other half is Joe. The teacher can 'conduct' the halves so that they can practise questions and answers.

Example 3: comparatives (lower intermediate)

Once again, the teacher may want to have students repeat a sentence or two to give them a chance to try out the new language. She may also feel that the students need practice of the individual word forms – the new comparatives. She can get choral and individual repetition of the words 'safer', 'more convenient' etc. and then ask students to say the sentence 'Trains are slower than planes'. She can then ensure quick practice by saying 'faster' to get students to say 'Planes are faster than trains', 'cheap' for 'Trains are cheaper than planes' etc.

To check that students have understood the meaning and the construction of comparative adjectives, she can ask them to make sentences comparing other things such as bicycles and cars using the adjectives from the lesson.

However, it is important to stress that with comparatives – as with any other language point – the amount of repetition (choral or individual) depends on how useful, enjoyable or comforting the students find it. The teacher could, for example, ask students to produce their own sentences straightaway and correct them appropriately so that they learn as they try the new language out.

Example 4: 'protection' (upper intermediate)

In the case of 'protection', it doesn't seem sensible to have students repeating sentences individually or in chorus. In the first place, the sentence is likely to be very long and long choruses are notoriously difficult to get right. In the second place, students at this level should know basic sentence construction and pronunciation anyway, so they are unlikely to need it. Lastly, students at this level may feel that repeating sentences in chorus (for example) is too unsophisticated for them.

A much better kind of practice is to ask them to make their own sentences using the word correctly. This often works best if they write sentences, since in this way they are given time to work things out. When they read back what they have written, the teacher can tell them if they are using the word correctly and appropriately.

Repetition does still have a use at this level despite what we have said. Students may still have problems pronouncing words – or working out how words should be pronounced just by looking at them. A quick chorus of 'environmental' or 'effective' can sometimes help to ensure that students start using these 'new' words correctly.

Why do students make mistakes?

All students make mistakes at various stages of their language learning. It is part of the natural process they are going through and occurs for a number of reasons. In the first place, the students' own language may get in the way. This is most obviously the case with 'false friends' – those words which sound or look the same but mean something different such as 'assistir' in Spanish which means 'attend' in English and not 'assist'. False friends are more common where the learner's language shares a common heritage with English (i.e. Romance languages).

Grammatical considerations matter too: Japanese students frequently have trouble with article usage, Germans have to get used to positioning the verb correctly, Arabic students have to deal with a completely different written system etc.

Interference from the students' own language is not the only reason for making mistakes. There is a category which a number of people call 'developmental' errors. These are the result of conscious or subconscious processing which frequently overgeneralises a rule, as, for example, when a student, having learnt to say things like 'I have to go', then starts saying 'I ~~must to go~~', not realising that the use of 'to' is not permitted with 'must'.

Some mistakes are deep-seated and need constant attention (ask experienced teachers about the third-person singular of the present simple!). While these are examples of 'errors', others seem to be more like 'slips' made while students are simultaneously processing information and they are therefore easier to correct quickly.

Whatever the reason for 'getting it wrong', it is vital for the teacher to realise that all students make mistakes as a natural and useful way of learning. By working out when and why things have gone wrong, they learn more about the language they are studying.

How should teachers correct students?

Correction helps students to clarify their understanding of the meaning and construction of language. It is a vital part of the teacher's role, and something which the teacher is uniquely able to provide, but precisely because it involves pointing out people's mistakes, we have to be careful when correcting since, if we do it in an insensitive way, we can upset our students and dent their confidence (see page 2). What is appropriate for one student may be quite wrong for another one.

In general, the teacher's job is to point out when something has gone wrong – and see if the student can correct herself or himself. Maybe what they said or wrote was just a slip and they are able to put it right straightaway.

Sometimes, however, students can't put mistakes right on their own, so we have to help them. We can do this by asking if one of their colleagues can help out or by explaining the problem ourselves.

If we get other students in the class to help out, we have to make sure that the student who made the mistake in the first place isn't going to be humiliated by this ('How come they all know the answer? I must be stupid!'). Sometimes, students like that prefer gentle correction from the teacher. On the other hand, in the right kind of atmosphere students enjoy helping each other – and being helped in return.

The following example shows students being corrected during the practice phase of the *Study* session on comparatives.

MONICA:	Trains are safer planes.
TEACHER:	Safer planes? (*with surprised questioning intonation*)
MONICA:	Oh ... Trains are safer than planes.
TEACHER:	Good, Monica. Now, 'comfortable' ... Simon?
SIMON:	Trains more comfortable. Planes are.
TEACHER:	Hmm. Can you help Simon, Bruno?
BRUNO:	Er ... Trains are more comfortable than planes.
TEACHER:	Thank you. Simon?
SIMON:	Trains are more comfortable than planes.
TEACHER:	That's right, Simon. Great. What about 'fast', Matilde?
MATILDE:	Trains faster planes.
TEACHER:	Trains are faster?
MATILDE:	Trains faster planes? I don't know.
TEACHER:	OK. Look. Trains go at a hundred miles an hour, planes go at 500 miles an hour, so planes are faster than trains. Yes?
MATILDE:	Planes are faster than trains.
TEACHER:	Well done, Matilde.

With Monica, all the teacher had to do was point out that something was wrong (by echoing what she said with a questioning intonation) and she immediately corrected herself. Simon was not able to do this, so the teacher got Bruno to help him. When Matilde made a mistake, however, (and was not able to correct herself) the teacher judged that she would be unhappy to have correction from her peers so she helped her out herself.

When organising practice, then, teachers need to listen out for mistakes, identify the problem and put it right in the most efficient and tactful way. As we shall see in Chapters 8 and 9, correction is a different matter when dealing with writing and speaking activities.

Before leaving the subject of correcting, it is worth pointing out that it is just one response that teachers can make to student language production. It is just as important – perhaps more so – to praise students for their success as it is to correct them when they fail. Teachers can show through the use of expression, encouraging words and noises ('good', 'well done', 'fantastic', 'mmm' etc.) that students are doing really well.

Where do language study activities fit in teaching sequences?

As we saw in Chapter 4, 'Study' is one element of the *'Engage-Study-Activate'* trinity. The elements can come in different orders and sequences depending on what is being studied as the following descriptions of our four language topics show.

Example 1: 'It's a pen' (complete beginners)

Engage

Study

Activate

> In our first example, the teacher is working with complete beginners. She starts by walking into the class, greeting the students in a lively and cheerful way. It is the first time she has seen them, so she tells them her name and, with a combination of mime and expression, gets them to tell her their names. Then she pantomimes finding an extraordinary object in her bag and holds up a pen as if it was the most interesting thing in the world. She has students repeat the word and then shows other objects which they learn the names of too. Then she demonstrates the sentences 'It's a pen/It's a table' and the students practise saying them. If she thinks they can take it, she introduces the question 'What is it?' and gets students practising asking and answering questions.
>
> As soon as she thinks they are ready, she gets them to role-play a scene in which two people wake up to find themselves in a darkened room. They have to find out what things in the room are by touch and asking 'What is it?' 'It's a desk ... wait ... and a pen ...' etc.

Example 2: invitations (elementary)

Engage

Activate

Activate

> The teacher gets students to say what their favourite evening activities are – where they like going out for example. She then shows them a picture of Joe and Sarah and asks 'Are they friends?' etc. to generate a (limited) discussion about their relationship.
>
> The teacher tells students they are going to listen to a tape. She asks them what they think it's about – based on the picture of Sarah and Joe. She tells them that all they have to do is say what Sarah wants and what Joe's reply is (she tells them to listen right to the end for this).
>
> The students listen to the tape more than once and then compare their answers in pairs before the teacher checks that they have understood that Sarah invites him to the cinema and Joe agrees – eventually.

(continued on the next page)

Study	The teacher tells them to listen again for the invitation language and then models it herself. She gets the students to repeat the new language and then practise it in pairs.
Study	Later, the teacher gives the students a written version of the whole conversation and with them she works on it as if she were a theatre director and the students were actors. They practise the scene in pairs and then some of the pairs act it out.
Activate	

Example 3: comparatives (lower intermediate)

Engage	The teacher tells a story about a journey she took that was terrible – things going wrong etc. Then she puts students in groups and tells them to find out what is the most and least favourite means of transport in each group. The groups report back to the class.
Activate	
Activate	The teacher selects two forms of transport and asks students to compare them (thus giving her a chance to see if any of them can already use comparatives).
Engage	The teacher now tells them to look at the title of the magazine article and asks them to speculate on what the article is going to be about. They then read the article and the teacher asks the students if they agree with the writer's opinions.
Activate	
Study	The students do the 'discovery' activity about comparative adjectives which we looked at on pages 58 and 61. They repeat comparatives sentences and make new ones.
Activate	Later, the teacher has them role-play a situation in which a customer goes into a furniture store to buy a new sofa/bed. As a result of this, the customer has to fax/phone his/her flatmate and describe the sofas and ask which one the flatmate thinks he/she should buy.

Example 4: 'protection' (upper intermediate)

Engage	Let us imagine that the students have been working on the subject of suntanning and burning etc. Now the teacher asks them whether or not they like advertisements and which their favourites are.
Activate	She then asks them to get into groups and discuss what concepts they would need to express if they were writing a radio advertisement about a new kind of sunscreen.

(continued on the next page)

Study

|

|

|

|

|

Activate

|

|

> After they have discussed this, she asks them for the concepts/words they have come up with in their groups and as a result offers them computer printouts of words like 'protection'. She asks the students to study them and work out how they occur in sentences (what comes before and after them). To check they've understood she gets them to write sentences using the new words/concepts. Finally, they get back into their groups and write their radio advertisements before recording them and playing them back to the rest of the class.

Conclusions

In this chapter we have
- said that students need to be exposed to language (in order to study it). They need to understand its meaning, understand its construction and practise it.
- seen that students can be exposed to language by the teacher using it for them to listen to/see, by listening to tapes, by reading texts and by looking at computer printouts. In each case, the students are given chances to see or hear the language before they are asked to produce it themselves.
- looked at many ways of making sure that students understand the meaning of words and grammar. Teachers can show objects, pictures and drawings. They can use mime, gesture and expression. They can use check questions to make sure students understand concepts. They can use time lines for verb tenses (for example) or explain meaning by listing opposite meanings. They can get more advanced students to write dictionary definitions and then compare them with the real thing.
- discussed the many ways in which we can help students to understand the construction of words and sentences including: isolating the 'bits' and saying them, demonstrating stress and intonation through exaggerated vocal delivery and the use of arm gestures, showing how forms are contracted using hands and fingers, writing tables on the board which make constructions clear or asking directed questions which prompt students to 'discover' facts about construction for themselves.
- talked about how teachers can get students to practise the language they are studying including choral or individual repetition, using prompt words to get students to make new sentences, asking students to practise questions and answers in pairs or asking students to write their own sentences.
- asked why students make mistakes and said that two main reasons are interference from their own languages and errors caused by their natural language development. Making mistakes and errors is part of the process of language learning.

- suggested that an important part of a teacher's job is to correct students when and if they make mistakes. Ideally, students will be able to correct themselves but if they can't, the teacher may do it or ask other students to help. However, we have to choose how to correct very sensitively.
- demonstrated how the *Study* parts of our model fit into teaching and learning sequences.

Looking ahead
- The next four chapters will look at what are often called 'the four skills' – reading, writing, speaking and listening – and will demonstrate the procedures we can use in each case.
- We will return to issues of language study in Chapter 11 on textbook use and Chapter 12 on lesson planning.

How to teach reading

- Why teach reading?
- What kind of reading should students do?
- What reading skills should students acquire?
- What are the principles behind the teaching of reading?
- What do reading sequences look like?
- More reading suggestions

Why teach reading?

There are many reasons why getting students to read English texts is an important part of the teacher's job. In the first place, many of them want to be able to read texts in English either for their careers, for study purposes or simply for pleasure. Anything we can do to make reading easier for them must be a good idea.

Reading is useful for other purposes too: any exposure to English (provided students understand it more or less) is a good thing for language students. At the very least, some of the language sticks in their minds as part of the process of language acquisition, and, if the reading text is especially interesting and engaging, acquisition is likely to be even more successful.

Reading texts also provide good models for English writing. When we teach the skill of writing, we will need to show students models of what we are encouraging them to do.

Reading texts also provide opportunities to study language: vocabulary, grammar, punctuation, and the way we construct sentences, paragraphs and texts. Lastly, good reading texts can introduce interesting topics, stimulate discussion, excite imaginative responses and be the springboard for well-rounded, fascinating lessons.

What kind of reading should students do?

There has been frequent discussion about what kinds of reading texts are suitable for English language students. The greatest controversy has centred on whether the texts should be 'authentic' or not. That is because people have worried about more traditional language-teaching materials which tended to look artificial and to use over-simplified language which any native speaker would find comical and untypical.

However, if you give low-level students a copy of *The Times* or *The Guardian* (which are certainly authentic for native-speakers), they will probably not be able to understand them at all. There will be far too many words they have never seen before, the grammar will be (for them) convoluted and the style will finish them off.

A balance has to be struck between real English on the one hand and the students' capabilities and interests on the other. There is some authentic written material which beginner students can understand to some degree: menus, timetables, signs and basic instructions, for example, and, where appropriate, we can use these. But for longer prose, we may want to offer our students texts which, while being like English, are nevertheless written or adapted especially for their level. The important thing is that such texts are as much like real English as possible.

The topics and types of reading text are worth considering too. Should our students always read factual encyclopedia-type texts or should we expose them to novels and short stories? Should they only read timetables and menus or can we offer them business letters and newspaper articles?

A lot will depend on who the students are. If they are all business people, the teacher may well want to concentrate on business texts. If they are science students, reading scientific texts may be a priority. But if, as is often the case, they are a mixed group with differing interest and careers, a more varied diet is appropriate. Among the things the teacher might want them to read are magazine articles, letters, stories, menus, advertisements, reports, play extracts, recipes, instructions, poems, and reference material.

What reading skills should students acquire?

Students, like the rest of us, need to be able to do a number of things with a reading text. They need to be able to *scan* the text for particular bits of information they are searching for. This skill means that they do not have to read every word and line; on the contrary, such an approach would stop them scanning successfully.

Students need to be able to *skim* a text – as if they were casting their eyes over its surface – to get a general idea of what it is about. Just as with scanning, if they try to gather all the details at this stage, they will get bogged down and may not be able to get the general idea because they are concentrating too hard on specifics.

Whether readers scan or skim depends on what kind of text they are reading and what they want to get out of it. They may scan a computer manual to find the one piece of information they need to use their machine, and they may skim a newspaper article to get a general idea of what's been happening. But we would expect them to be less utilitarian with a literary work where *reading for pleasure* will be a slower, closer kind of activity.

Reading for detailed comprehension, whether looking for detailed information or language, must be seen by students as something very different from the reading skills mentioned above. When looking for details, we expect students to concentrate on the minutiae of what they are reading.

One of the teacher's main functions when training students to read is not only to persuade them of the advantages of skimming and scanning, but also to make them see that the way they read is vitally important.

What are the principles behind the teaching of reading?

Principle 1: *Reading is not a passive skill*.

Reading is an incredibly active occupation. To do it successfully, we have to understand what the words mean, see the pictures the words are painting, understand the arguments, and work out if we agree with them. If we do not do these things – and if students do not do these things – then we only just scratch the surface of the text and we quickly forget it.

Principle 2: *Students need to be engaged with what they are reading*.

As with everything else in lessons, students who are not engaged with the reading text – not actively interested in what they are doing – are less likely to benefit from it. When they are really fired up by the topic or the task, they get much more from what is in front of them.

Principle 3: *Students should be encouraged to respond to the content of a reading text, not just to the language*.

Of course, it is important to study reading texts for the way they use language, the number of paragraphs they contain and how many times they use relative clauses. But the meaning, the message of the text, is just as important and we must give students a chance to respond to that message in some way. It is especially important that they should be allowed to express their feelings about the topic – thus provoking personal engagement with it and the language.

Principle 4: *Prediction is a major factor in reading*.

When we read texts in our own language, we frequently have a good idea of the content before we actually read. Book covers give us a hint of what's in the book, photographs and headlines hint at what articles are about and reports look like reports before we read a single word.

The moment we get this hint – the book cover, the headline, the word-processed page – our brain starts predicting what we are going to read. Expectations are set up and the active process of reading is ready to begin. Teachers should give students 'hints' so that they can predict what's coming too. It will make them better and more engaged readers.

Principle 5: *Match the task to the topic*.

We could give students Hamlet's famous soliloquy 'To be or not to be' and ask them to say how many times the infinitive is used. We could give them a restaurant menu and ask them to list the ingredients alphabetically. There might be reasons for both tasks, but, on the face of it, they look a bit silly. We will probably be more interested in what Hamlet means and what the menu foods actually are.

Once a decision has been taken about what reading text the students are going to read, we need to choose good reading tasks – the right kind of questions, engaging and useful puzzles etc. The most interesting text can be undermined by asking boring and inappropriate questions; the most commonplace passage can be made really exciting with imaginative and challenging tasks.

Principle 6: *Good teachers exploit reading texts to the full.*

Any reading text is full of sentences, words, ideas, descriptions etc. It doesn't make sense just to get students to read it and then drop it to move on to something else. Good teachers integrate the reading text into interesting class sequences, using the topic for discussion and further tasks, using the language for *Study* and later *Activation*.

What do reading sequences look like?

In the following four examples, we are going to look at four different kinds of reading texts and four different kinds of reading tasks. In each case we will see how the reading text fits into an *ESA* sequence.

Example 1 (elementary)

In the first example for elementary students, the teacher has introduced the topic of 'attraction'. He asks the students what they find attractive in a person. With luck, the discussion of the topic should be enjoyable and amusing.

He then tells the students they have to fill in the following chart about what their partner thinks is important when he or she meets a new friend.

	very important	important	not very important
physical appearance			
clothes			
job or education			
family			
money and possessions			
personality or character			
religion			
politics			
other ...			

The students now have to list the qualities in order of importance for them as a whole class. The teacher then tells the class to read the text on the next page to see how their opinions are different from the men and women being described.

When the students have read the text, the teacher allows them to discuss their answers in pairs. This is to give them a chance to clear up any small comprehension problems before they talk in front of the class.

The students now have to complete the following task.

Read the first part of the article again. Use these words to answer the questions below.
eyes   legs   face   smile   figure   teeth

Which do men think are most important?
Which do women think are the most important?
Do you agree?

THE MAIN ATTRACTION

Suddenly it happens. You just know he's the man for you, and you haven't even been introduced yet. But how do you know? And can you make sure he feels the same way? *Company* **investigates...**

What first attracts men to women? Whereas women tend to notice the eyes, teeth and smile in particular, men will be more likely to assess the face in general and pay more attention to figure and legs.

According to a recent survey by *Singles* magazine, these are the top ten attributes that men and women look for in each other, in order of priority

Men look for a woman who is:
- attractive
- sincere
- slim
- a non-smoker
- with a sense of humour
- affectionate
- tall
- kind

Women look for a man who is:
- tall
- professional
- with a sense of humour
- attractive (not necessarily handsome)
- sincere
- intelligent
- handsome
- kind

From *the Beginners' Choice* by Sue Mohamed and Richard Acklam

As a follow-up to these reading tasks, the teacher asks the students to think of people who they find attractive (friends, film stars, athletes etc.). They are then asked to say what the most attractive thing about them is. The discussion can lead on to descriptive writing etc.

Notice that this patchwork lesson started with an *Engage* activity, then went on to an *Activate* exercise (working with a partner), followed by an *Activate* reading (do you agree with the passage?), a *Study* reading (answer the questions) before being followed up with *Activate* exercises.

Notice, too, how important the first *Activate* exercise was: it gave the students a chance to predict what was coming.

Example 2 (lower intermediate)

In the second example, the class is once again prepared for the reading by discussing what, if anything, the students know about ghosts. The teacher may get them to say whether they believe in ghosts or not and if they have ever seen one.

After that, the textbook from which this reading text is taken gives students some information about ghosts (that they are usually the result of a tragic death, that they appear at night etc.).

The students are now asked to read the text on page 74 to say whether Orcas Manor is a typical haunted house. This is a general reading task designed to let them get an overall picture of the text.

For the next reading, the students are asked more detailed *Study*-type questions, e.g.

Complete the table

Which ghost	He killed	You can see him in ... .
1 previous owner		
2	visitors	
3		the corridors
4		

From *Language in Use* by Adrian Doff and Chris Jones

The students can check their answers in pairs before the teacher puts the chart on the board and has individuals come out and fill it in to check that the whole class have understood the text.

SANDFORD ORCAS MANOR

Dorset, England

Next to the church in the village of Sandford Orcas there is an old gatehouse. If you go through the gate you arrive at the sinister manor house which is famous for its large number of ghosts.

The present owner of the manor says that it is difficult to keep servants because the ghosts frighten them. Many people have seen the ghost of the previous owner. He was a farmer who committed suicide by hanging himself from the gatehouse, and he often appears in the garden wearing old working clothes.

Another ghost is an 18th century priest who used to kill visitors while they were asleep in their beds. He still sometimes frightens guests in the middle of the night by standing over their beds holding a knife.

The ghost of a servant sometimes walks along the dark corridors of the house. He murdered his master at Sandford Orcas, but nobody knows why.

But perhaps the most frightening story is of a young man who grew up in the house and then became a sailor. While he was at sea, he killed a boy, and then went mad. When he returned to Sandford Orcas, they locked him in a room at the back of the house. He never left the room again, and died there several years later. On some nights when the moon is full, you can hear him screaming and banging on the door of the room.

From *Language in Use* by Adrian Doff and Chris Jones

The teacher wants students to understand how we use pronouns to refer back to subjects we have already mentioned. He asks them who or what 'it', 'them' and 'He' refer to in paragraph two. What do 'they', 'their', 'He' refer to in paragraph three?

As a follow-up task, students can write a description of a haunted house which they can invent. They can do this individually or in pairs or groups. They can read out their final versions to the rest of the class.

Once again, a patchwork lesson has started with an *Engage* session where teacher and students talk about haunted houses and read some information about ghosts. Then they read for general understanding – an *Activate* type of exercise – before *Studying* the text – both for meaning and then for language use (personal pronoun use in text writing) – and then doing another *Activate* follow–up.

Example 3 (intermediate)

In this example for intermediate students, the students first look at a picture of people sunbathing and say whether it is a positive, safe and attractive image – or whether it is the opposite.

They are then shown the following magazine article.

POLLY GRIFFITHS GOES DOWN TO THE SEA FOR ADVICE ON HOW TO LOOK GOOD AND STAY SAFE.

So you think you're too pale and want to get a good suntan this summer? Why not? Except that unless you're careful the sun can make your skin old and leathery and can even give you skin cancer.

If you must sunbathe (and let's face it, lots of us think it's a good idea), then have a look at these gorgeous guys and babes I found on the beach and see which of them is like you.

ROGER
I'm the type who always burns. It's because I'm fair-skinned - and I've got red hair and freckles. That's why I'm so good-looking! But I still burn unless I use a really high SPF (sun protection factor) - about 20 in strong sun.

JEAN
Yeah I tan easily. People like me who are dark-skinned (with dark hair and brown eyes) are not only really cool but we go even browner in the sun. I still use a sunscreen though, something light with an SPF of about 6 ...

MELINDA
I have to be careful 'cause I'm the type who burns easily. But I do tan in the end. If you've got fair hair and blue eyes like me you'd better use quite a strong sunscreen (an SPF of 15 to start with) ...

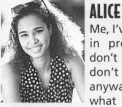

ALICE
Me, I've got built-in protection! I don't burn, but I don't sunbathe anyway. I mean what for? I like messing around on the beach, though.

SO THE MESSAGE IS: CHECK OUT WHAT KIND OF SKIN YOU'VE GOT AND THEN BE SAFE AND SENSIBLE – AND HAVE A GOOD TIME! SEE YOU AT THE POOLSIDE BAR!

The teacher checks that they have understood by asking them questions like 'What sun protection factor does Roger use?' 'Does Melinda burn?' 'Who is dark-skinned, fair skinned?' etc. Students then use language from the article to describe themselves.

In this straight arrows lesson, the teacher starts by *Engaging* the students with discussions of sunbathing. They then *Study* the text before going on to *Activate* the knowledge which the text has given them.

Example 4 (intermediate to advanced)

The final example shows that reading does not have to be a static activity dealing with prose passages. We can make it much more dynamic than that.

The teacher wants to get his intermediate students reading poetry, both because he thinks they will enjoy it (if done in an *Engaging* way) and because he thinks it can provide a useful focus for language study.

He asks students if they like poetry. Can they remember any poems? What are they about? What do poets normally write about?

He tells them that he is going to put students in groups of nine. Each student in the group will get a line from a poem. They can read it aloud but they must not show it to the other eight members of the group. The task of the group is to put the lines in the right order for the poem.

He then hands out the following lines (at random) to the nine members of the group.

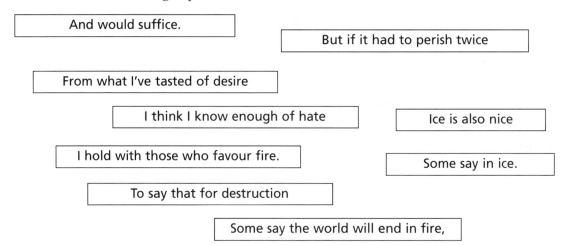

And would suffice.

But if it had to perish twice

From what I've tasted of desire

I think I know enough of hate

Ice is also nice

I hold with those who favour fire.

Some say in ice.

To say that for destruction

Some say the world will end in fire,

They read their lines out to each other and see if they can put them in the right order. Ideally, the groups will be standing up in circles so that the members can change position when the group have decided where their lines come in the poem.

As the activity goes on, the teacher goes round the groups listening to how they are getting on. If they are not making any headway, he may prompt them by saying 'Shall I tell you what the first line is?' or 'Think of the sounds of the last word in each line' etc.

When the students (think they) have finished the task, the teacher reads the poem aloud for them to check their versions. This is what he reads:

Some say the world will end in fire,
Some say in ice.
From what I've tasted of desire
I hold with those who favour fire.
But if it had to perish twice
I think I know enough of hate
To say that for destruction
Ice is also nice
And would suffice.

The groups have to decide on a good title for the poem which they can then compare with the original (which is 'Fire and Ice' – the poem is by Robert Frost).

The teacher can then ask students to say whether they like the poem and whether they think it is funny, sad, serious or tragic. He then gets them to describe the rhyme scheme of the last words in each line (A, B, A, A, B, C, D, B, B).

The teacher then gives students first lines of poems and tells them to write their own (he can make it 'the worst poem in the world' competition to bring in humour) using a particular rhyme scheme, for example.

This reading activity works because students really have to *Engage* with the meaning and construction of the poem. When they are trying to put the poem in order, you will hear them discussing rhymes, punctuation, logic and word meaning. It is popular with students (if used only occasionally), even with those who are not natural fans of poetry. Interestingly, after an initial *Engage* session, it quickly becomes a perfect mixture of *Study* and *Activation* – studying the poem's construction whilst still activating all the language they know.

More reading suggestions

1   Students read small ads for holidays, partners, things for sale etc., to make a choice. They amplify the ads into descriptions. (intermediate/ advanced)

2   Students read jumbled instructions for a simple operation (using a public phonebox etc.) and have to put the instructions in the correct order. (elementary/ intermediate)

3   Students read a recipe and after matching instructions with pictures, they have to cook the food! (elementary/intermediate)

4   Students read an extract from a play or film and, after ensuring that they understand it, they have to work on acting it out. (any level)

5   Students are given a number of words from a text. In groups, they have to predict what kind of a text they are going to read. They then read the text to see if their original predictions were correct. (elementary/intermediate)

6   Students have to match topic sentences with the paragraphs they come from. (intermediate/upper intermediate)

7   Students read a text and have to guess which of a group of people they think wrote the text (using the pictures provided). (lower intermediate/advanced)

8   Students read a narrative with the end missing. In groups, they have to supply their own ending. (intermediate/advanced)

9   Students read a 'factfile' about a country, population, machine or process etc. They have to convert the information into bar graphs or pie charts. (intermediate/advanced)

Conclusions   In this chapter we have

- talked about the reasons for using reading texts in class: for language acquisition, as models for future writing, as opportunities for language study and, of course, for practice in the skill of reading.
- discussed the balance that has to be reached between genuinely authentic material (written for fluent native speakers) and material specially designed for students. We have talked about the need for topics and reading types depending on who the students are.
- said that students need to know the difference between *scanning* and *skimming*. They need to realise how to read for different purposes – including *reading for pleasure* and *reading for detailed comprehension*.
- come up with six reading 'principles': reading is not a passive skill, students need to be *Engaged* while they are reading, students need to be *Engaged* with the content of a text, not just its language, prediction is a major factor in reading, the task needs to be matched to the topic, and good teachers exploit reading texts to the full.
- looked at four reading sequences showing the use of *Engage* and *Activate* exercises for prediction, and the need for follow-up activities. We have seen one example where the main reading activity (combining *Study* and *Activating*) is more like a puzzle.

Looking ahead

- The teaching of reading is intimately bound up with the teaching of writing: the one provides the model for the other. We will look at writing in the next chapter.
- Many of the issues related to reading are similar to listening issues - as we will see in Chapter 10.

How to teach writing

- Why teach writing?
- What kind of writing should students do?
- What do writing sequences look like?
- How should teachers correct writing?
- What can be done about handwriting?
- How does writing fit into *ESA*?
- More writing suggestions

Why teach writing?   The reasons for teaching writing to students of English as a foreign language include reinforcement, language development, learning style and, most importantly, writing as a skill in its own right. We will look at each of these in turn.

Reinforcement: some students acquire languages in a purely oral/aural way, but most of us benefit greatly from seeing the language written down. The visual demonstration of language construction is invaluable for both our understanding of how it all fits together and as an aid to committing the new language to memory. Students often find it useful to write sentences using new language shortly after they have studied it.

Language development: we can't be sure, but it seems that the actual process of writing (rather like the process of speaking) helps us to learn as we go along. The mental activity we have to go through in order to construct proper written texts is all part of the ongoing learning experience.

Learning style: some students are fantastically quick at picking up language just by looking and listening. For the rest of us, it may take a little longer. For many learners, the time to think things through, to produce language in a slower way, is invaluable. Writing is appropriate for such learners. It can also be a quiet reflective activity instead of the rush and bother of interpersonal face-to-face communication.

Writing as a skill: by far the most important reason for teaching writing, of course, is that it is a basic language skill, just as important as speaking, listening and reading. Students need to know how to write letters, how to put written reports together, how to reply to advertisements – and increasingly, how to write using electronic media. They need to know some of writing's special conventions (punctuation, paragraph construction etc.) just as they need to know how to pronounce spoken English appropriately. Part of our job is to give them that skill.

What kind of writing should students do?

Like many other aspects of English language teaching, the type of writing we get students to do will depend on their age, interests and level. We can get beginners to write simple poems, but we probably won't give them an extended report on town planning to do. When we set tasks for elementary students, we will make sure that the students have – or can get – enough language to complete the task. Such students can write a simple story but they are not equipped to create a complex narrative. It's all a question of what language the students have at their command and what can be achieved with this language. As we shall see with the four examples in this chapter, the models we give students to imitate will be chosen according to their abilities.

In general, however, we will try to get students writing in a number of common everyday styles. These will include writing postcards, letters of various kinds, filling in forms such as job applications, writing narrative compositions, reports, newspaper and magazine articles etc. We may also want to have students write such text types as dialogues, playscripts, advertisements, or poems – if we think these will motivate them.

Another factor which can determine our choice of writing task is the students' interests. If everyone in the class works in a bank, we might choose to get them writing bank reports. If they are all travel agents, you can imagine getting them to write alluring advertisements for special deals. But, of course, this should not preclude using other types of creative writing with such groups.

When we have a much more mixed group – students, secretaries, doctors, teachers and police officers, for example – their interests won't be so easy to pin down. At this point we will choose writing tasks which we think are generally useful but which, more importantly, they are likely to enjoy doing. Students may never have a need to write a scene from a soap opera, for example, but they might enjoy having a go, so it is worth doing.

There is no limit to the kinds of text we can ask students to write. Our decisions, though, will be based on how much language the students know, what their interests are and what we think will not only be useful for them but also motivate them as well.

What do writing sequences look like?

The four examples of writing we are going to look at show a range of level and complexity.

Example 1: postcards (elementary)

In this example at the elementary level, students *Study* a particular type of writing and then write something which is very similar in design and structure to what they have just been looking at.

The teacher starts by having students look at this postcard.

We're staying at a lovely hotel near the beach. We get up late every day and have a large breakfast. Then we lie around all morning, swimming and reading. After lunch – siesta! Then it's more swimming and a late supper. Paradise!
Tomorrow we're going to Isla Mujeres (Island of the Women).
See you soon,

Love
Mary

Judy Saunders

6 Turtas Road,

Cambridge CT5 3YR

INGLATERRA

The teacher checks that the students understand the information in the card and then she asks them to identify four different patterns in it: the present continuous ('We're staying at a lovely hotel ...'), the present simple ('We get up late every day ...'), verbless sentences, postcard style ('After lunch – siesta!') and present continuous for future ('Tomorrow we're going ...').

The students then discuss the fact that, in postcards, greetings (like 'Dear Judy') are not necessary. Signings-off are informal ('Love Mary').

Now that students have examined the structure of the postcard, the teacher asks them to imagine that they too are on holiday. They must decide where. She tells them that they, too, must send a postcard to an English-speaking friend. Like the example postcard, they should say where they are, what they do every day, what they're doing tomorrow/next week etc., and they should sign off informally.

When the students have completed the task, the teacher can collect the postcards and correct them later (see below page 84) or the students can read them out, or they can show their cards to other people.

This postcard activity is an example of 'parallel writing' – where students stick closely to a model they have been given, and where the model guides their own efforts. It is especially useful for the kind of formulaic writing represented by postcards, certain kinds of letters, announcements and invitations, for example.

Example 2: altering dictations (intermediate)

In this activity, the teacher dictates statements which students have to alter to suit their own preferences and priorities. It is a writing activity which is especially useful during a lesson sequence which is designed to ask people to take positions on a certain subject – and can therefore be used as a prelude to a discussion, or a controversial reading, for example.

The teacher tells students she is going to dictate a number of sentences. However, the students should change the sentences as she dictates them so that they reflect their own points of view. In other words, the sentence they write down will be an amended form of the sentence the teacher starts with. As an example the teacher reads this sentence.

Human beings do not treat animals well.

and tells students to re-write the sentence to suit their own feelings. She may read this original sentence more than once and she then gives students time to complete their sentences. Here are examples of what students might write:

Some people think that human beings do not treat animals well, but I do not think this is very important.

Human beings must treat animals better because they are living creatures too.

The teacher then reads out more sentences, giving students adequate time to alter them, e.g.

The way people treat animals tells you what kind of people they are.
There is no difference between killing animals for food and killing people in war.
If all the world was vegetarian, we'd all be a lot happier.

The students then compare what they have written in pairs or groups before reading them out to the class. The teacher only corrects where there are glaring errors. Alternatively, pairs and groups could be asked to pool their sentences and come up with a new one which represents a fair compromise between the various points of view.

The finished sentences either then lead into a reading or listening text about vegetarianism – or they may form the start of a discussion activity (see Chapter 9).

Example 3: newspaper headlines/articles (intermediate)

In this sequence, the teacher introduces students to the way newspaper headlines are constructed and then gets students to write their own newspaper articles. The sequence starts when the teacher asks the students if they read newspapers, and what they read about. They have a short discussion. The teacher then gets students to match newspaper headlines with the stories they came from, as in the following example.

1 Match the newspaper headlines with the stories they came from.

a

Neighbour slams rock party

i At the monthly meeting of the housing committee of Barkingside district council, chairman Geoffrey Caspar resigned dramatically when his opposite number Glenda Beckett

b

Housing chief quits at stormy meeting

ii When his neighbours played loud music until three in the morning Philip Mitchell (82) went mad. "I couldn't stand it any more," he said. "I'm an old man and I need

- The teacher now elicits the facts that, for example, headlines frequently use the present simple tense and invariably leave out articles and auxiliaries. She might point out that there is special vocabulary for headlines (e.g. 'slams' for 'complains about', 'quits' instead of 'leaves').
- Students are then asked to choose one of the following topics: a disaster, a neighbourhood quarrel, a resignation/sudden departure of a public figure, a sports triumph, a scandal involving a public figure (actor, politician etc.). In pairs, they have to think of a short story to go with the topic they have chosen.
- The pairs now write the headlines for their stories and write them up on the board for the rest of the class — who have to guess what the story is about. The teacher can suggest changes, corrections and amendments to the headlines during this stage of the lesson.
- The students then write articles to go with the headlines. While they are doing this, the teacher goes round the class offering them help when and if they need it.
- The teacher can stick the articles up on the class noticeboard or, if this is not possible, have students read their stories out to the rest of the class.
- Newspaper writing can be used in a number of different ways. In this example, for instance, when pairs have made up a headline they can give it to another pair who have to use it to invent a story of their own. Or perhaps all the headlines could be detached from their newspaper articles so that a new matching exercise could take place.

Example 4: report writing (advanced)

In this example for an upper intermediate or advanced level class, the writing task forms part of a much longer project-like sequence. The teacher is going to get students to write a report about leisure activities.

The teacher introduces the topic and asks students to give her any words they associate with leisure activities. She writes them on the board and adds any of her own that she thinks the students need.

She then asks students to design a questionnaire which will find out how people spend their leisure time (see pages 89-90 for the use of questionnaires as speaking activities). When they have collected the information they need through their questionnaires, they discuss how they are going to write the report. This is where the teacher will introduce some of the features of report writing that are necessary for the task, e.g. 'In order to find out how people spend their leisure time we ...' or 'One surprising fact to emerge was that ...' and 'The results of our survey suggest that ...' etc. As with many examples of writing style, the teacher can suggest ways in which the text should be constructed (what comes in the introduction, middle paragraphs and conclusion) and offer language which the writing style uses (as in our report-writing example above).

The students now draft their reports which the teacher collects to correct. When she hands them back, the students write them up in final form and show them to their colleagues to see if they all said more or less the same thing.

How should teachers correct writing?

Most students find it very dispiriting if they get a piece of written work back and it is covered in red ink, underlinings and crossings-out. It is a powerful visual statement of the fact that their written English is terrible.

Of course, some pieces of written work are completely full of mistakes, but even in these cases, over-correction can have a very demotivating effect. As with all types of correction, the teacher has to achieve a balance between being accurate and truthful on the one hand and treating students sensitively and sympathetically on the other.

One way of avoiding the 'over-correction' problem is for teachers to tell their students that for a particular piece of work they are only going to correct mistakes of punctuation, or spelling, or grammar etc. This has two advantages: it makes students concentrate on that particular aspect, and it cuts down on the correction.

Another technique which many teachers use is to agree on a list of written symbols (S = spelling, WO = word order etc). When they come across a mistake they underline it discreetly and write the symbol in the margin. This makes correction look less damaging.

However many mistakes you may want to identify, it is always worth writing a comment at the end of a piece of written work – anything from 'Well done' to 'This is a good story, but you must look again at your use of past tenses – see X grammar book page 00'.

Two last points: correcting is important, but it can be time-consuming and frustrating, especially when it is difficult to know what the mistake is because it is unclear what the student is trying to say. Common sense and talking to students about it are the only solutions here. The other really important point is that correction is worthless if students just put their corrected writing away and never look at it again. Teachers have to ensure that they understand the problem and then redraft the passage correctly.

What can be done about handwriting?

Handwriting is a very personal matter. It is supposed to reflect character. Different nationalities certainly have recognisable handwriting traits. Some people have easily readable writing. Some produce written work which is indecipherable, whether beautiful or messy and ugly.

Many nationalities do not use the same kind of script as English, so for students from those cultures writing in English is doubly difficult: they are fighting their expressive limitations as well as trying to work out a completely new writing system at the same time. And now that word processors are becoming more and more common, people have less motivation for good handwriting.

Teachers are not in a position to ask students to change their handwriting style, but they can insist on neatness and legibility. Especially when students are heading towards an exam, such things are crucial. With students who are having problems with English script, special classes or group sessions may have to be arranged to help them. In these classes they can be shown many examples of certain letters, and the teacher can demonstrate the strokes necessary for making those shapes – and where the letter starts (writing from left to right is difficult for some students). They can be asked to write 'in the air' to give them confidence or they can be asked to imitate letters on lined paper which demonstrates the position and height of letters, e.g.

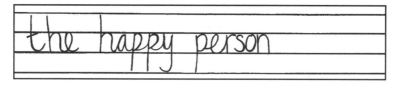

How does writing fit into *ESA*?

The four writing examples in this chapter approach the *ESA* procedure from a number of different angles. In the case of the postcard the teacher may first talk to students about postcards and/or holidays in such a way as to *Engage* them. They then *Study* the postcard looking for typical 'postcard features' and finally they *Activate* that knowledge by writing their own version.

In the 'altering dictations' activity, the students are, hopefully, *Engaged* by the dictation and topic of the sentence they write down. When they alter the sentence they are *Activating* the knowledge of English which they have. After the discussion (*Activate*) which this will provoke, the teacher will give feedback on the language used, making corrections where appropriate (*Study*).

A different kind of boomerang procedure is evident in the newspaper-writing activity. Students are first *Engaged* with the topic of newspapers before doing the matching task (*Activate*). They then *Study* headlines before going on to a creative writing stage (*Activate*).

In report writing, a number of stages are gone through, giving the whole sequence a patchwork feel. Students need to be *Engaged* with the topic, they need to *Study* the language which they will need, knowledge which is *Activated* in the collection of results before students come back to study the structure of reports in order to produce a final piece of work *(Activation)*.

More writing suggestions

1 Students write letters to a newspaper in response to a controversial article. (intermediate/advanced)
2 Students expand a variety of headlines into newspaper articles. (intermediate/advanced)
3 Students write/design their own menus. (beginner/lower intermediate)
4 Students design posters for a party/play/concert etc. (beginner/lower intermediate)
5 Students write a radio news bulletin. (elementary/intermediate)

6   Students write a letter of application for a job. (any level)
7   Students write the description of a room while listening to music. (intermediate)
8   Students send e-mail messages (real or simulated) to other English speakers around the world. (any level)
9   Students write invitations of various kinds. (elementary/intermediate)

Conclusions   In this chapter we have

- looked at the reasons for teaching writing: reinforcement of learnt language, the development of the students' language through the activity of writing, the appropriacy of the activity of writing for some styles of learning and the importance of writing as a skill in its own right.
- said that what students write will depend on level and the motivational effect of the task. In general, students should practise writing postcards, letters, forms, narratives, reports and articles – as well as (perhaps) more frivolous tasks.
- studied four writing sequences.
- tackled the difficult subject of correcting writing, suggesting that over-correction should be avoided and that teachers should always strive to be encouraging.
- pointed out that, while handwriting is a matter of style, teachers should expect students to write clearly and legibly. In some cases, students may need special help in the shaping of letters, for example.

Looking ahead

- The next two chapters are about the spoken word. They mirror many of the comments made about reading and writing.
- After that comes Chapter 11 on textbook use, a vital teacher skill, and then Chapter 12 on lesson planning.

How to teach speaking

- What kind of speaking should students do?
- Why encourage students to do speaking tasks?
- What do speaking activities look like?
- How should teachers correct speaking?
- What else should teachers do during a speaking activity?
- How do speaking activities fit into *ESA*?
- More speaking suggestions

What kind of speaking should students do?

It is important to be clear about the kind of speaking this chapter is talking about. We are not going to look at controlled language practice where students say a lot of sentences using a particular piece of grammar or a particular function, for example. That kind of speaking belongs in Chapter 6 and is connected with *Study*. The kind of speaking we are talking about here is almost always an *Activate* exercise (see Chapter 4). In other words, the students are using any and all the language at their command to perform some kind of oral task. The important thing is that there should be a task to complete and that the students should want to complete it.

Why encourage students to do speaking tasks?

There are three basic reasons why it is a good idea to give students speaking tasks which provoke them to use all and any language at their command.

Rehearsal: getting students to have a free discussion gives them a chance to rehearse having discussions outside the classroom. Having them take part in a role-play at an airport check-in desk allows them to rehearse such a real-life event in the safety of the classroom. This is not the same as practice in which more detailed study takes place; instead it is a way for students to 'get the feel' of what communicating in the foreign language really feels like.

Feedback: speaking tasks where students are trying to use all and any language they know provides feedback for both teacher and students. Teachers can see how well their class is doing and what language problems they are having (that is a good reason for 'boomerang' lessons); students can also see how easy they find a particular kind of speaking and what they need to do to improve. Speaking activities can give them enormous confidence and satisfaction, and with sensitive teacher guidance can encourage them into further study.

Engagement: good speaking activities can and should be highly motivating. If all the students are participating fully – and if the teacher has set up the activity properly and can then give sympathetic and useful feedback – they will get tremendous satisfaction from it. Many speaking tasks (role-playing, discussion, problem-solving etc) are intrinsically enjoyable in themselves.

What do speaking activities look like?

In the following four examples, we are going to look at very different speaking activities, from puzzle-like tasks to more involved role-playing. All the activities satisfy the three reasons for speaking tasks which we mentioned above.

Example 1: information gaps (elementary/intermediate)

One type of speaking activity involves the so-called 'information gap' – where two speakers have different parts of information making up a whole. Because they have different information, there is a 'gap' between them.

One popular information-gap activity is called 'Describe and Draw'. In this activity one student has a picture which he or she must not show his or her partner (teachers sometimes like to use surrealist paintings – empty doorways on beaches, trains coming out of fireplaces etc). All the partner has to do is draw the picture without looking at the original, so the one with the picture will give instructions and descriptions, and the 'artist' will ask questions.

Describe and Draw has many of the elements of an ideal speaking activity. It is highly motivating (if used only very occasionally), there is a real purpose for the communication taking place (the information gap, completion of the task), and almost any language can be used. Remember to swap the students' roles around if the activity is used more than once, so that the describer becomes the drawer and vice-versa.

A further extension of the information gap idea occurs in the following story-telling activity.

The teacher puts the class into four groups, calling them A, B, C and D. To each group he gives one of the following pictures.

From *Touchdown for Mexico* by Jeremy Harmer, D'Arcy Adrian Vallance and Olivia Johnston

The groups have to memorise everything they can about the pictures – who's in them, what's happening etc. They can talk about the details in their groups.

The teacher now collects back the pictures and asks for one student from each group (A, B, C and D) to form a new four-person group. He tells them that they have each seen a different picture but that the pictures taken together – in some order or other – tell a story. The task is for the students to work out what the story is. The only way they can do this is by describing their pictures to each other and speculating on how they are connected.

The final stories may be different. The groups tell the whole class what their version is, and the teacher can finally re-show the pictures.

This story-telling activity can, of course, be used as a prelude to written narrative work.

Example 2: surveys (elementary)

One way of provoking conversation and opinion exchange is to get students to conduct questionnaires and surveys. If the students plan these questionnaires themselves, the activity becomes even more useful.

In this example for elementary students, the present perfect tense has recently been introduced. The teacher wants students to activate all their language knowledge and would be only too happy if this provoked natural use of the present perfect.

The topic is sleep – ways of sleeping, sleeping experiences etc. First of all, the teacher talks about sleep. Perhaps he tells a story about not being able to sleep, about a nightmare, or about someone he has seen sleepwalking. He gets students to give him as much 'sleep' vocabulary as they can (e.g. 'dream', 'nightmare', 'walk in your sleep', 'heavy sleeper', 'light sleeper'). The students now work in pairs to plan questions for their sleep questionnaire and the teacher goes round helping where necessary.

A simple student questionnaire might end up looking like this:

SLEEP QUESTIONNAIRE

- *How many hours do you normally sleep?* ....

- *Are you a light sleeper/ heavy sleeper?* ....

- *Have you ever*

	yes	**no**
talked in your sleep?	☐	☐
walked in your sleep?	☐	☐
had a nightmare?	☐	☐
fallen out of bed?	☐	☐

If you answer yes, describe the experience (s):

....

....

....

The students go round the class questioning other students and noting down what they say. While they are doing this, the teacher listens and prompts where necessary and he then gets them to tell the class of any interesting experiences they have uncovered before moving on to remedial language work that may be necessary (see *How should teachers correct speaking?* on page 94).

Encouraging students to get up and walk around talking to other classmates (not only the ones they are sitting next to) has many advantages. It varies the structure of classroom periods, allows people a bit of physical movement, and provides a welcome variety of interaction.

Students can design and use surveys and questionnaires about any topic – smoking, TV watching, feelings and emotions, transport, musical preferences etc. They are often a good lead-in to writing work.

Example 3: discussion (intermediate/upper intermediate)

Most teachers hope that they will be able to organise discussion sessions in their classroom, particularly if the exchange of opinions provokes spontaneous fluent language use. Many find, however, that discussion sessions are less successful than they had hoped.

The first thing to remember is that people need time to assemble their thoughts before any discussion. The ability to give spontaneous and articulate opinions is challenging in our own language, let alone the language we are struggling to learn. The following sequence, therefore, stresses the need for discussion preparation and shows the teacher building the discussion up in stages.

The teacher starts by asking individual students to name the last film they saw. Did they enjoy it? Was it funny? Serious? Violent? The replies he gets at this point will be fairly monosyllabic, but at least the topic has been introduced and the students are enjoying thinking about movies.

The teacher now says that the class is going to concentrate on the issue of violence in films. Is there too much? Does it matter? Should anything be done about it? He puts the students into groups. In one group, the students have to think (and make notes about) the level of violence in films and what effects it might have. In another group, students have to think of (and make notes about) ways of stopping the portrayal of violence in films. In another group, students have to think up (and make notes about) reasons why the level of violence in films is quite justifiable and unworrying.

When students have had a chance to think of ideas (with the teacher going round to individual groups offering help where necessary), he asks for an opinion about violence from one of the groups. When a student has given it, he encourages other students to ask questions about that opinion. He then asks a different student to say what can be done about it, and that student, in turn, is questioned. Finally he asks a student from the 'violence isn't worrying' group to disagree with the idea that violence in movies is a bad thing.

The teacher keeps prompting in this way until the conversation takes off, with different opinions being freely exchanged. Later, when the activity has run out of steam, he can work on any language arising out of the activity.

This kind of discussion can be formalised into a proper debate – speakers on different sides giving speeches, comments from 'the floor' and a vote at the end. It can also be provoked by giving pairs statements they have to assess on a 0 (= completely disagree) to 5 (= completely agree) scale for, e.g.

There's too much violence in movies. 0 1 2 3 4 5

or by giving the class a number of different statements. They have to choose one and defend it.

There are many discussion possibilities. The important thing is that students need to be *Engaged* with the topic. They then might do some *Study* (if there is a necessity for language input, facts or figures, for example) and move quickly to *Activate* stages – which include the discussion itself. Almost certainly, however there will be feedback, including *Study*, after the discussion is over.

Example 4: role-play (upper intermediate/advanced)

Role-play activities are those where students are asked to imagine that they are in different situations and act accordingly. We may tell them to role-play being guests at a party, travel agents answering customer questions or participants in a public meeting about a road-building project for example. Role-play activities provide the kind of rehearsal possibilities we discussed at the beginning of this chapter.

In the following example, a meeting is being held to decide whether a new supermarket should be built on land which is currently used as school playing fields. Students are put into groups of six. Each student is given the following card.

Homefield college, a teacher training establishment, is running short of money. It wants to sell half of its playing fields to the Taksi supermarket chain. The chairperson of the city planning committee has called a meeting to discuss the issues raised. At the meeting are the chairperson, Colin Grafter (a representative from Taksi), local residents Muriel Fightwell and Brian Shelfsurch, and Councillors Clare Howe-Sing and Amby Valent.

The students decide who is who in each group and the teacher then hands out the following cards to the individuals, with the instruction that they should read them but not show them to anyone else. This is what the cards show.

Chairperson

It is your job to run the meeting and make sure everyone's voice is heard. Start by getting everyone to introduce themselves by name and say what their occupation is. Ask them to state their point of view, but at all stages allow other members to question them. At the end of the meeting, you will call for a vote on the supermarket project.

Colin Grafter, Taksi representative

You represent Taksi. You are offering an important facility for the public. You will pay for a new slip road from Taksi's funds and you will make the new supermarket attractive with adequate parking and play areas for children.

Muriel Fightwell, local resident

You love the playing fields and frequently walk there with your dog. The last thing your area needs is a new supermarket with hundreds more cars clogging up the streets, and polluting the air for the families around, not to mention the destruction of a beautiful piece of land in the heart of a residential area.

Brian Shelfsurch, local resident

You welcome the idea of a new supermarket. The nearest one is four miles away and in the rush hour (when you normally do your shopping) it takes hours to get there. This new scheme will be just right for your own shopping needs – and since Taksi have agreed on a new road it shouldn't cause too much of a problem.

Councillor Clare Howe-Sing, local politician

You do not think the council should agree to this use of the land when there is a shortage of low-cost accommodation for the city's residents. If the land is to be sold by the college, it should be used for building flats and houses for low-income tenants – that's what the council's priority should be.

Councillor Amby Valent

You are sympathetic to both sides of the argument. You think the supermarket would benefit locals, but you don't want to see the loss of green spaces. You will decide which way to vote when you have heard the discussion (you should ask as many questions as necessary to help you decide).

The teacher tells students that they can ask him about any details they are not sure of. He tells them that they must stick to the information on their original cards, but that they can invent new facts which fit with that information.

The teacher now tells the groups to start, but sets a time limit for the chairperson to announce the result of the vote. While the activity is going on, the teacher goes round the groups prompting where necessary and making notes on examples of good and bad English usage that he hears.

When the time limit is up, the teacher asks the various chairpeople to say how their groups voted and why. This can lead into a discussion about resolving different demands on land use, for example. The teacher then gives the students feedback: what he heard and was impressed by; what mistakes he heard which he thinks they might all benefit from concentrating on.

The role-play can now lead into a number of possible writing tasks: a segment of the dialogue, a newspaper report on the decision, letters to the newspaper, posters and newsletters from the anti-Taksi campaign etc.

Two things can be added to this description. Firstly, the teacher could make the role-play a whole-class activity by having all the students act out a public meeting with many speakers. This might be very enjoyable but would cut down on the amount of speaking time for each individual. But it would at least make the voting more unpredictable, and you could build in 'public' question sessions at various stages of the meeting.

Secondly, not all role-plays need to be this intricate. If you ask your students to role-play a party situation, for example, all you might need to do is set the party scene and then tell students to go either as themselves – or as a living or dead person they would like to be!

Role-play is more than just play-acting: it offers chances for rehearsal and *Engagement* that some other activities fail to give.

How should teachers correct speaking?

It is important for teachers to correct mistakes made during speaking activities in a different way from the mistakes made during a *Study* exercise. When students are repeating sentences trying to get their pronunciation exactly right, then the teacher will often correct (appropriately) every time there's a problem (see Chapter 6). But if the same teacher did the same thing while students were involved in a passionate discussion about whether smoking should be banned on tourist beaches, for example, the effect might well be to destroy the conversational flow. If, just at the moment one of the students is making an important point, the teacher says 'Hey wait, you said "is" but it should be "are", beaches are ... repeat', the point will quickly be lost. Constant interruption from the teacher will destroy the purpose of the speaking activity.

Many teachers watch and listen while speaking activities are taking place. They note down things that seemed to go well and times when students couldn't make themselves understood or made important mistakes. When the activity has finished, they then ask the students how they thought it went before giving their own feedback. They may say that they liked the way Student A said this and the way Student B was able to disagree with her. They will then say that they did hear one or two mistakes and they can then either discuss them with the class, write them on the board or give them individually to the students concerned. In each case, they will ask the students to see if they can identify the problem and correct it.

As with any kind of correction, it is important not to single students out for particular criticism. Many teachers deal with the mistakes they heard without saying who made them.

Of course, there are no hard and fast rules about correcting. Some teachers who have a good relationship with their students can intervene appropriately during a speaking activity if they do it in a quiet non-obtrusive way. But it is a risky enterprise. The general principle of watching and listening so that you can give feedback later is usually much more appropriate.

What else should teachers do during a speaking activity?

Some teachers get very involved with their students during a speaking activity and want to join in too! They may argue forcefully in a discussion or get fascinated by a role-play and start 'playing' themselves.

There's nothing wrong with teachers getting involved, of course, provided they don't start to dominate. Although it is probably better to stand back so that you can watch and listen to what's going on, students can also appreciate teacher participation at the appropriate level – in other words, not too much!

Sometimes, however, teachers will have to intervene in some way if the activity is not going smoothly. If someone in a role-play can't think of what to say, or if a discussion begins to dry up, the teacher will have to decide if the activity should be stopped – because the topic has run out of steam – or if careful prompting can get it going again. That's where the teacher may make a point in a discussion or quickly take on a role to push a role-play forward.

Prompting is often necessary but, as with correction, teachers should do it sympathetically and sensitively.

How do speaking activities fit into *ESA*?

The speaking activities in this chapter tend to follow the same basic pattern: *Engage-Activate-Study* – that is, the teacher gets students interested in the topic, the students do the task while the teacher watches and listens and they then study any language issues that the teacher has identified as being problems. So, in one sense, these are classic boomerang sequences such as the ones we discussed in Chapter 4.

Some commentators like to talk about *opportunistic* teaching – that is, the desirability of teaching a piece of language which only becomes apparent as a result of something going on in the class. Thus, it may become clear that students have not been able to use some language that would have been helpful during an *Activate* stage – or which might be helpful for something they are doing right now. The teacher uses this as an ideal opportunity to suddenly decide – opportunistically – to bring forward some new language for study because it 'seemed like a good idea at the time'. The boomerang starts to look more like a patchwork.

A mistake some teachers make is to think that, once a piece of language has been studied, a good speaking activity will immediately cement it in students' minds. This is not always the case. Most teachers will tell you that it usually takes a bit of time, a few lessons, before 'new' language comes out in fluency activities. Today's speaking activity may be provoking students into using language they first learnt some time ago.

Speaking activities may well form one part of a much longer sequence which includes reading or listening and, after the activity, *Study* work. We will often use such activities simply to provide welcome relief from more formal work.

More speaking suggestions

1 Students work in pairs. One has a number of elements (e.g. pictures) arranged in a certain way. The other student has the same elements, but loose, and has to arrange them in the same way by talking to his partner without looking at the partner's picture/plan. This is called 'Describe and Arrange'. (elementary/ intermediate)

2 Students, in pairs, each have similar pictures, but with differences. Through talking to each other, they have to 'find the differences' without looking at each other's pictures. (elementary/intermediate)

3 Students make a list of the kind of things that people like or do (e.g. go jogging, brush teeth five times a day etc.). They have to go round the class to 'find someone who' does, did, likes etc. those things. (any level)

4 Students think of five famous people. They have to decide on the perfect gift for each person. (any level)

5 Students in groups look at five different photographs. They have to decide which one should win a photographic prize. The groups then have to agree with each other to come to a final decision. (intermediate/advanced)

6 Students role-play a formal/business social occasion where they meet a number of people and introduce themselves. (elementary/any level)

7 Students give a talk on a given topic and/or person. (advanced)

8 Students conduct a 'balloon debate' where only one person can stay in the balloon and they have to make their case as to why they should be the one. (upper intermediate/advanced)

9 Students are presented with a 'moral dilemma' – e.g. a student is caught cheating in an important exam. Given the student's circumstances, which of five possible courses of action should be followed? Groups reach a consensus. (intermediate/advanced)

Conclusions

In this chapter we have
- said that speaking activities perform an *Activate* rather than a *Study* function.
- seen how speaking activities provide opportunities for rehearsal, give both teacher and students feedback and motivate students because of their *Engaging* qualities.
- looked at examples of four types of speaking activity: information gap, survey, discussion and role-play.
- discussed the way teachers should correct in speaking activities, not interrupting while they are going on, but giving feedback later.
- suggested that there may be times when teachers need to help an activity along through prompting (and perhaps participation) provided it is done sensitively.
- decided that speaking activities typically follow a boomerang or patchwork pattern.

Looking ahead

- The next chapter looks at speaking's mirror: listening. After that, we will discuss textbook use and lesson planning, two essential teacher skills.
- In Chapter 13 *What if?* we look at various problem situations, including three that concern speaking activities especially: What happens if students use their own language rather than English? What can we do with students who are reluctant to speak? What happens if some groups finish earlier than others?

How to teach listening

- Why teach listening?
- What kind of listening should students do?
- What's special about listening?
- What are the principles behind the teaching of listening?
- What do listening sequences look like?
- Where does video fit in?
- More listening suggestions

Why teach listening?

One of the main reasons for getting students to listen to spoken English is to let them hear different varieties and accents – rather than just the voice of their teacher with its own idiosyncrasies. In today's world, they need to be exposed not only to one variety of English (British English, for example) but also to varieties such as American English, Australian English, Caribbean English, Indian English or West African English. When people of different nationalities speak to each other, they often use English too, so that a Swiss flight attendant might well have to understand a Japanese woman's English variety, just as an Argentinian might need to be able to cope with a Russian's version.

There are, of course, problems associated with the issue of language variety. Within British English, for example, there are many different dialects and accents. The differences are not only in the pronunciation of sounds ('bath' like 'laugh' vs 'bath' like 'cat') but also in grammar (the use of 'shall' in northern varieties compared with its use in 'Standard English' – the southern, BBC-type variety; the grammatically coherent use of 'done', e.g. 'I done it' in non-standard English). The same is of course true for American, Indian or West African English.

Despite the desirability of exposing students to many varieties of English, however, common sense is called for. The number of different varieties (and the degree to which they are different from the one students are learning) will be a matter for the teacher to judge, based on the students' level, where the classes are taking place etc. But even if they only hear occasional (and very mild) varieties of English which are different from the teacher's, it will give them a better idea of the world language which English has become.

The main method of exposing students to spoken English (after the teacher) is through the use of taped material which can exemplify a wide range of topics such as advertisements, news broadcasts, poetry reading, plays, (pop) songs with lyrics, speeches, telephone conversations and all manner of spoken exchanges. Teachers can imitate these, but good tapes are far more powerful.

The second major reason for teaching listening is because it helps students to acquire language subconsciously even if teachers do not draw attention to its special features. As we have said in Chapter 4, exposure to language is a fundamental requirement for anyone wanting to learn it. Listening to appropriate tapes provides such exposure and students get vital information not only about grammar and vocabulary but also about pronunciation, rhythm, intonation, pitch and stress.

Lastly, just as with reading, students get better at listening the more they do it! Listening is a skill and any help we can give students in performing that skill will help them to be better listeners.

What kind of listening should students do?

The debate about the use of authentic listening material is just as fierce in listening as it is in reading. If, for example, we play a tape of a political speech to complete beginners, they won't understand a word. You could argue that such a tape would at least give them a feel for the sound of the language, but beyond that it is difficult to see what they would get out of it. If, on the other hand, we give them a realistic (though not authentic) tape of a telephone conversation, they may learn much more about the language – and start to gain confidence as a result.

Listening demands listener engagement, too. Long tapes on subjects which students are not interested in at all will not only be demotivating, but students might well 'switch off' – and once they do that it becomes difficult for them to tune back into the tape. Comprehension is lost and the listening becomes valueless.

Everything depends on level, and the kind of tasks that go with a tape. There may well be some authentic material which is usable by beginners such as pre-recorded announcements, telephone messages etc. More difficult material may be appropriate for elementary students provided that the questions they are asked do not demand detailed understanding. Advanced students may benefit from scripted material provided that it is interesting and subtle enough – and provided the tasks that go with it are appropriate for their level.

Since, as we have said, listening to tapes is a way of bringing different kinds of speaking into the classroom, we will want to play different kinds of tape to them, e.g. announcements, conversations, telephone exchanges, lectures, 'plays', news broadcasts, interviews, other radio programmes, stories read aloud etc.

What's special about listening?

There are a numbers of ways in which listening activities differ from other classroom exercises: firstly, tapes go at the same speed for everybody. Unlike language study or speaking practice – or even reading, where individual students can read (to some extent) at their own pace – the tape continues even if individual students are lost. Unlike reading, listeners to a tape cannot flick back to a previous paragraph, re-read the headline, stop to look at the picture and think for a bit before continuing. On the contrary, they have to go with the speed of the voice(s) they are listening to. Of course, they can stop tapes and rewind them, but, essentially, the speed of the speaker(s) dominates the interaction, not that of the listener.

It is perhaps this relentlessness of taped material which accounts for the feeling of panic which many students experience during listening activities. If they fail to recognise a word or phrase they haven't understood – and if, therefore, they stop to think about it – they often miss the next part of the tape and are soon falling behind in terms of comprehension. It is especially for this reason that students have to be encouraged to listen for general understanding first rather than trying to pick out details immediately. They must get into the habit of letting the whole tape 'wash over them' on first hearing, thus achieving general comprehension before returning to listen for specific detail.

Listening is special too because spoken language, especially when it is informal, has a number of unique features including the use of incomplete utterances (e.g. 'Dinner?' serving as a perfectly functional way of asking 'Is dinner ready?'), repetitions (e.g. 'I'm absolutely sure, absolutely sure you know that she's right'), hesitations ('Yes, well, ummm, yes, possibly, but, er ...') etc. Experience of informal spoken English together with an appreciation of other spoken factors – the tone of the voice, the intonation the speakers use, rhythm, and background noise – will help students to tease meaning out of such speech phenomena.

Because of its special characteristics, teachers need to ensure that students are well prepared for listening and that they are clearly able to hear what they listen to. These and other concerns are summarised in the following six principles.

What are the principles behind the teaching of listening?	**Principle 1:** *The tape recorder is just as important as the tape.*

What are the principles behind the teaching of listening?

Principle 1: *The tape recorder is just as important as the tape.*

However good your tape is, it will be useless if the tape recorder has a poor speaker or if the motor speed keeps changing and the tape goes faster or slower. You need to be sure that the tape recorder can be heard all round the classroom.

Another vital feature is a tape counter that is easy to see. When you find the right place on the tape, you can either remember the number which the counter is showing or press the counter at that point so that it now shows 000. In both cases, you can find your way back when you want to play the tape for the second or third time – instead of going backwards and forwards all the time trying to find the right place. With longer tapes, you can also note the counter number for each part or section you may need to return to.

Remember too that if you want to use your tape recorder for music as well as speech you may need a better machine.

Principle 2: *Preparation is vital.*

Teachers and students need to be prepared for listening because of the special features we discussed above.

Teachers need to listen to the tape all the way through before they take it into class. That way, they will be prepared for any problems, noises, accents etc., that come up. That way, they can judge whether students will be able to cope with the tape and the tasks that go with it.

Students need to be made ready to listen. This means that they will need to look at pictures, discuss the topic, or read the questions first, for example, to be in a position to predict what is coming. Teachers will do their best to get students *Engaged* with the topic and the task so that they really want to listen.

Principle 3: *Once will not be enough.*

There are almost no occasions when the teacher will play a tape only once. Students will want to hear it again to pick up the things they missed the first time. You may well want them to have a chance to study some of the language features on the tape.

The first listening is often used just to give students an idea of what the listening material sounds like (see Principle 5) so that subsequent listenings are easier for students. Once students have listened to a tape two or three times, however, they will probably not want to hear it too many times more.

Principle 4: *Students should be encouraged to respond to the content of a listening, not just to the language.*

As with reading, the most important part of listening practice is to draw out the meaning, what is intended, what impression it makes on the students. Questions like 'Do you agree?' are just as important as questions like 'What language did she use to invite him?'

Principle 5: *Different listening stages demand different listening tasks.*

Because there are different things we want to do with a listening text, we need to set different tasks for different listening stages. This means that, for a first listening, the task needs to be fairly straightforward and general (and almost certainly of the *Activate* type). That way, the students' general understanding and response can be successful – and the stress associated with listening can be neutralised.

Later listenings, however, may focus in on detail – of information, language use, pronunciation etc.

Principle 6: *Good teachers exploit listening texts to the full.*

If teachers ask students to invest time and emotional energy in a listening task – and if they themselves have spent time choosing and preparing the listening – then it makes sense to use the tape for as many different applications as possible. Thus, after an initial play of a tape, the teacher can play it again for various kinds of *Study* before using the subject matter, situation or tapescript for a new activity. The listening then becomes an important event in a teaching sequence rather than just an exercise by itself.

In the following four examples, we are going to look at listening activities from beginner to upper intermediate levels. Although the tapescripts are all different, the sequences have one thing in common: they *Engage* the students, before preparing them with a brief *Study* phase to face the listening phase.

Example 1 (beginners)

Before the listening takes place, the students have been introduced to (and practised saying) words like 'coffee', 'tea', 'breakfast' etc. They have done a quick question-and-answer drill with 'What do you have for breakfast?'

They now look at three photographs: a woman at the counter of a café giving her order, a woman in an office holding a coffee pot and (apparently) offering coffee to a man, and a woman at a restaurant table being attended to by a waiter.

The students look at the pictures and say what they are (a café, an office and a restaurant). They are then asked to listen to three conversations. All they have to do is match the conversations to the pictures (e.g. 'Conversation 1 is in ...'). When the teacher has made sure they understand the task, she plays them these tapes.

Conversation 1
WAITER: Good morning, madam.
WOMAN: Good morning. An English breakfast, please.
WAITER: Tea or coffee?
WOMAN: Tea, please.

Conversation 2
WOMAN: Cup of coffee?
CLIENT: Oh yes, please. That'd be lovely.
WOMAN: Sugar?
CLIENT: Just one, please.

Conversation 3
CUSTOMER: A tea, 2 black coffees and an orange juice, please.
WAITER: Anything else?
CUSTOMER: No, thank you.

From *the Beginner's Choice* by Sue Mohamed and Richard Acklam

The first task has allowed students to listen to the tapes with only a very general (and fairly straightforward) task to perform. Now they are going to listen in more detail.

Listen again. Tick (√) the drinks they have.

conversation	1	2	3
coffee tea hot chocolate orange juice	√		

A further listening asks the students to say how many drinks the people had.

The students are now in a position to role-play offering and accepting various kinds of drink. The role-play is a good follow-up to the listening task.

Notice how the sequence moves from preparation to general language practice followed by attention to detail (twice), finishing with a follow-up task. The whole sequence shows a patchwork lesson in operation from the early *Engage-Study-Engage-Activate* sequence (students learning new words and then speculating about the content of pictures). Their first listening is more like an *Activate* stage than anything else, and, as they move into greater focus on detail, *Studying* takes over. A final *Activate* role-play finishes off the lesson.

Example 2 (elementary)

In this example, the listening leads into grammar work which focuses on some of the language which has been heard on the tape.

The extract is part of a running storyline and the taped dialogue is consciously theatrical – much like a radio drama or a soap opera. The students see the textbook page on page 103.

The students read and listen to the paragraphs about the people in the photographs. Then they ask (and answer) questions about the people in the pictures.

CLASSIC ENGLISH

Who are they?

Tony Stuart is a waiter. He works in a restaurant in Oxford. He is tall and thin. He's got dark hair. He's twenty-four years old and he loves a beautiful young woman. Her name is Juliet. She's got long, fair hair and he thinks she is very beautiful. Her father is very rich.

Maureen Murphy is thirty years old. She works in a museum in Oxford. She is tall and has got fair hair.

Basil Newton hasn't got very much hair now. It's grey. He isn't tall and he isn't short. He's fifty-five years old and he's Juliet's father.

Harry is thirty-one years old. He's got short, dark hair. He isn't fat but he isn't very thin. He's married to Maureen.

1 Look at the people in picture one. Which questions can you answer about them?

1 What are their names?
2 How old are they?
3 What can you say about their hair?
4 What does one of them do?

Now talk about the people in the other pictures. What can you say about them?

2 Listen to two people.

1 Who are the two people?
2 One of the two people says "I don't want to talk about him". Who is 'him'?
3 Does she like him?
4 Does she love him?

From *Classic English* by Robert O'Neill with Gaynor Ramsey

103

Now that they are familiar with the scenes and are *Engaged* with the topic (through the work they are doing and the teacher's encouragement) the teacher gets them to look at the questions in exercise 2. The students are asked whether they can predict the answers. Then they listen to the tape. This is what they hear.

BASIL: Well? Do you? Do you love him?
JULIET: I don't want to talk about him.
BASIL: But I want to talk about him. Now answer my question, Julia.
JULIET: Why do you want to know?
BASIL: Because I'm your father, that's why. Do you love him?
JULIET: I like him very much.
BASIL: That isn't an answer to my question.
JULIET: No.
BASIL: No? What does that mean?
JULIET: No, I don't love him, Daddy. But he loves me.
BASIL: Do you see him very often?
JULIET: No, not very often. He works in the evening.
BASIL: He works in the evening? What does he do?
JULIET: He's a waiter, Daddy.
BASIL: A waiter!
JULIET: Yes, Daddy. He's a waiter in a restaurant. He's a very nice boy. But I don't love him!

The teacher gives students a chance to check through their answers together (to give them confidence) before going through the answers. She may play the tape again if they have had problems.

The teacher will go on to *Study* the language of physical description in the text, the use of pronouns in the dialogue etc. The listening practice part of the lesson has helped to move the story (and the topic) on.

Apart from the language work, the teacher can also get students to look at the tapescript and act out the dialogue as an *Activate* stage.

Example 3 (intermediate)

This example shows how listening practice can be integrated into a topic sequence.

The sequence starts by getting students to try and match cultural practices (people asking how much you earn, the importance of saying no to offers of second helpings, using the right hand only for handling food, not looking your superiors in the face) with various countries. They then decide which of the customs they would find it most difficult to get used to.

Clearly, we hope that the students will be *Engaged* by this discussion as well as becoming interested in the topic of cultural difference. They are also well prepared for the subject matter of the forthcoming listening. They look at the following task.

You will hear someone talking about something that happened to him in the Sudan. The story is in three parts.

Part 1
- What was he doing?
- How many people were there?
- What did they start doing?
- What do you think the speaker did next?

Part 2
- What did everyone eat?
- Why do you think they didn't eat the tomatoes?

Part 3
- Why didn't they eat the tomatoes?

The teacher gets the students to speculate about what they're going to hear – can they predict the story from the question clues? It's obviously something to do with something the speaker did with tomatoes. It's something to do with food and cultural issues. It takes place in the Sudan. Can they guess what they will hear?

They are now ready to listen. The teacher stops the tape after each part to allow students to compare answers with each other. This is especially important after the second part to allow them time to predict what the tomato problem was. Here is what they hear.

I was travelling in the Sudan by train and the journey I had to make was going to last about 48 hours and about an hour into the journey someone in my compartment, I think there were another seven people in the compartment, someone spread a large cloth on the floor and people began to bring food. No-one had a knife, so people were breaking up the food and placing it on the cloth ... .

I realised that this was the thing to do so all I had was three or four tomatoes. So I broke up my tomatoes and put them on the cloth and then we all started to eat the food. And there was bread and beans and lamb and many different things and people were eating and I noticed that no-one was eating my tomatoes. So I encouraged them to eat and everyone smiled very politely but wouldn't actually take any. And slowly the food disappeared and disappeared and my tomatoes were left. So at the end of the meal there was nothing left except my tomatoes. And I felt slightly uneasy about this, I didn't know why ... .

I thought probably it was because I was a foreigner and perhaps the Sudanese people didn't want to take a foreigner's food from them. So in fact I ate the tomatoes myself. It was only some time later that I realised that in fact the reason that people hadn't eaten my tomatoes was because I had broken up the tomatoes with both hands.

From *Language in Use Intermediate* by Adrian Doff and Christopher Jones

The tapescript provides good evidence of the use of different past tenses (past simple, past continuous, 'would', 'I realised I was', 'I thought it was' etc.) and the teacher can get students to listen again to identify examples of these, filling in a chart for each category.

As a follow-up, students can talk about times when they have misunderstood cultural symbols. Or they can talk about the advice they would give a foreigner coming to visit their country: What things should the visitor absolutely not do?

The sequence has here provided opportunities for an *Engage-Activate* pattern leading back to a *Study* session on the language mentioned above before following up with a discussion *Activate* stage.

Example 4 (upper intermediate)

In this example for upper intermediate students, the teacher is faced with the problem of wanting to use a long taped segment which is complex and contains much of the (perhaps problematic) speech phenomena we discussed in Chapter 4. It will be especially important, therefore, for the students to be properly prepared for listening.

The teacher starts by asking the students to put the following sports in order from 1 (= most frightening/challenging) to 10 (= least frightening).

hang-gliding scuba-diving parachuting downhill-racing
motor-racing mountaineering ski-jumping horse-riding
motorcycle-racing boxing

When the students have done this, the whole class can discuss which are the frightening sports and why. This *Engage* and *Activate* session is preparing students to tackle a particular topic.

The students are told that they are going to hear a British ski-jumper talking. He is going to tell them how he injured himself some years ago. They are told to read the following three summaries.

a) Eddie Edwards was working for a schools group in Italy. An Italian skier raced him downhill. The prize was to take a girl out to dinner. At the bottom of the mountain the Italian took a corner sharply and crashed into Eddie, who was hurt badly. Later, Eddie married the girl and now they have two children.

b) Eddie Edwards was in a downhill race in Italy. The prize was the job of ski technician for a school group. He was racing an Italian skier downhill. At the bottom of the mountain he took a corner sharply, flew into the air and crashed into a girl spectator. He was hurt badly, but later asked the girl out to dinner.

c) Eddie Edwards was working as a ski technician with a school group in Italy. An Italian skier raced him downhill. The prize was to invite a girl out to dinner. At the bottom of the mountain Eddie took a corner sharply, flew into the air, crashed into the Italian and then fell against rocks, hurting himself badly.

The teacher checks that they understand the summaries and then tells them that only one of them is correct. As they listen they have to decide which one it is. This is what they hear.

Interviewer: In your skiing and in the jumping you've injured yourself a number of times, haven't you?

Eddie: Oh gosh, yes.

Interviewer: What sort of things have you done to yourself?

Eddie: In Italy, when I ... I raced a guy ... he was the local champion and he was ranked sixth in Italy for downhill at the time, and I just went out to work for a company called 'Schools Abroad', a travel company that dealt specifically with schools, colleges, um, all youth groups of all ages I think ... um, and I worked for them as a ski technician and that allowed me to work for about two hours a week and I'd ski eight hours a day seven days a week, you see; and after about a month I was getting pretty good, 'cos I was a good skier anyway but after spending about two months out on the snow I was getting really hot and er, so everybody started to hear about this Englishman who was getting on really well at the skiing and getting really fast and things, and then this local guy came up to me – he was getting on for about twenty-six I think but he was really ...

Interviewer: Very old.

Eddie: Very old, yeah, I mean ancient! But he was the super-hot skier of the whole sort of country and er he came up to me and offered me a race, you see, and we said that ... 'cos he was having a bit of a, let's say a flirt with the rep of Schools Abroad who was there with me. And she was a nice-looking girl, a blonde and all this sort of thing, so I said OK, but I'll race you and the winner can take the girl out – June, her name was – so the winner ... we'd go from the top of the mountain to the bottom and the winner could take her out to dinner, you see; and so we went up to the mountain one day, up to the top. We went straight away first thing in the morning so that we knew there was nobody down the slope because that was the most important – we didn't want to, we didn't mind killing ourselves, but we didn't want to kill anybody else – and so we got to the top. All the er lift guys were at the bottom watching and all the ski school; and for a few days beforehand they were saying, 'Don't race him, don't race him he'll hammer you, you know, you'll get hurt,' all this sort of thing, 'you haven't got a .. you can't stand a chance,' and all this sort of thing. So we took off together at the top of the mountain and we were going down, and he was just in front of me by about ten metres but it wasn't it wasn't a great deal, and I knew I could catch it up any time so I just sort of stuck behind him. And we were doing about seventy, seventy-five miles an hour and we were coming towards the bottom and on the ... at the bottom there was a left-hand bend going into the finish but on this bend there was a ridge, you see. Now if you took this bend nice and long on the outside it was only a slight ridge and you wouldn't take off but the sharper you took the bend the bigger the ridge so the further you would fly in the air, you see. And I was catching my this guy up; we were about two metres, within two metres two metres of each other so I decided I'd take the bend a little bit sharper than him; so I took off, was going towards the finish but er going in the air and I was going across the slope and so er ... you know although I was in control I couldn't do anything until I landed obviously; and we were doing about seventy miles an hour and I landed right on top of him and er as soon as I hit him my skis released. I didn't have a helmet on, and I hit him, skis released, and I went over and I was rotating sideways but still travelling about seventy miles an hour. I didn't know where I was and then all of a sudden I had a great thump on the back of my head and er I hit rocks and went into trees and all sorts of things, and er they rushed me off to hospital with a suspected broken neck, broken back, and I paralysed my shoulder and arm; and er he didn't finish either so nobody won ...

Interviewer: So she didn't get to have any dinner.

Eddie: No. In fact now they're married and they've got two kids!

From *The Listening File* by Jeremy Harmer and Steve Elsworth

The students compare their answers and decide that the correct summary is (**c**). The teacher now asks them to listen again, only this time they are reporters and their editor has asked them to find out details about Eddie's job, who was skiing that day, what the witnesses thought, what the cause of the accident was and what injuries Eddie suffered.

When this listening is over (and a subsequent one if necessary) the teacher asks the students to complete one of the following tasks.

– Eddie rings his dad to ask for some money for his hospital bill.
– Eddie is asked to make the speech at the Italian's wedding reception.
– You are a reporter who is asked to interview Eddie Edwards.
– You have read about Eddie and the Italian's race in the newspaper. You object strongly.

This whole procedure – starting with *Engage* and *Activate* stages and ending up with *Activation* – allows students to tackle a tape they would otherwise find difficult. It maximises the tape (we could add gap-filling exercises etc. for *Study* work) and ends with a useful selection of follow-up tasks.

Where does video fit in?

Almost everything we have said about listening applies to video too. We have to choose video material according to the level and interests of our students. If we make it too difficult or too easy, the students will not be motivated. If the content is irrelevant to the students' interest, it may fail to engage them.

Video is richer than audio tape. Speakers can be seen. Their body movements give clues as to meaning, so do the clothes they wear, their location etc. Background information can be filled in visually.

Some teachers, however, think that video is less useful for teaching listening than audio tape precisely because, with the visual senses engaged as well as the audio senses, students pay less attention to what they are actually hearing.

A danger of video is that students might treat it rather as they treat watching television – e.g. uncritically, lazily. For this (and other) reason(s) teachers have developed a number of special techniques for videos such as the following.

Playing the tape without sound: students and teacher discuss what they see, what clues it gives them and then they guess what the characters are actually saying. Once they have predicted the conversation, the teacher rewinds the video and plays it with sound. Were they right?

Playing the tape but covering the picture: this reverses the previous procedure. While the students listen, they try to judge where the speakers are, what they look like, what's going on etc. When they have predicted this, they listen again, this time with the visual images as well. Were they correct?

Freezing the picture: the teacher presses the pause button and asks the students what's going to happen next. Can they predict?

Dividing the class in half: half the class face the screen. The other half sit with their backs to it. The 'screen' half describe the visual images to the 'wall' half.

There are many more video techniques, of course. See pages 183-4 for more on video.

Many teachers use video. It brings an extra dimension to the class and can be most enjoyable. Used carelessly, however, it soon loses any special quality and becomes instead a kind of second-rate television.

More listening suggestions

1 In three groups, students listen to three different tapes (witness reports, phone conversations arranging a meeting etc). By comparing notes, they have to work out the truth. This is called 'jigsaw listening'. (intermediate/advanced)

2 Students listen to a phone message being given. They have to record the message on a message pad. (elementary)

3 Students hear sound effects. They use them to construct a story of what actually happened. (elementary)

4 Students listen to a narrative and have to plot the characters' movements on a map. (elementary/upper intermediate)

5 Students listen to a news broadcast and compare it with a newspaper report. What are the differences? (upper intermediate/advanced)

6 Students listen to three poems being read by three different people. They have to choose a mood/colour for each and say which they like best. (intermediate/advanced)

7 Students listen to people describing their occupations. They have to decide what the people look like and what the occupations are. (intermediate/upper intermediate)

8 Students listen to a story. They have to put some pictures in the correct order to match the story. (elementary/intermediate)

9 Students listen to a recorded message of films, times and prices etc., and decide which film they are going to see when. (elementary/ intermediate)

Conclusions   In this chapter we have
- discussed the reasons for using listening in the classroom – the need to expose students to different varieties of English, and different kinds of listening. We talked about the benefit to language acquisition.
- said that the needs, levels and interests of the students will determine the kind of listening that teachers use. Although it should always be realistic, it may not always be absolutely 'authentic'.
- examined the reasons why listening is different, in particular the fact that speech goes at the speaker's, not the listener's speed.
- provided six principles for listening: the tape recorder is just as important as the tape, preparation is vital, once will not be enough, students should be encouraged to respond to the content of the listening, not just the language, different listening stages demand different listening tasks, good teachers exploit listening texts to the full.
- looked at four listening sequences showing how preparation is a major part of the sequence, and showing how listening leads on to follow-up tasks.
- discussed where video fits in, mentioning some video techniques and stressing that using video is not an excuse for TV watching.

Looking ahead
- The next two chapters show how to exploit textbooks to the full and what to think about when planning a lesson.
- In Chapter 13 *What if?* we look at various problem situations, including what happens if students just don't understand the taped material in a listening class.

How to use textbooks

- What are the different options for textbook use?
- What do adding, adapting and replacing look like?
- So why use textbooks at all?
- How should teachers choose textbooks?

What are the different options for textbook use?

When teachers open a page in their textbook, they have to decide whether they should use the lesson on that page with their class. Is the language at the right level? Is the topic/content suitable for the students? Are there the right kind of activities in the book? Is the sequencing of the lesson logical?

If the language, content and sequencing of the textbook are appropriate, the teacher will want to go ahead and use it. If, however, there is something wrong with the textbook, the teacher has to decide what to do next. (We will discuss the general issue of textbook advantages and disadvantages on pages 116-7.)

In his book *Making the Most of Your Textbook*, the author Neville Grant suggests four alternatives when the teacher decides the textbook is not appropriate. Firstly, he or she might simply decide to *omit* the lesson. That solves the problem of inappropriacy and allows him or her to get on with something else.

There's nothing wrong with omitting lessons from textbooks. Teachers do it all the time, developing a kind of 'pick and choose' approach to what's in front of them. However, if they omit too many pages, the students may begin to wonder why they are using the book in the first place, especially if they have bought it themselves.

Grant's second option is to *replace* the textbook lesson with one of the teacher's own. This has obvious advantages: the teacher's own material probably interests him or her more than the textbook and it may well be more appropriate for the students. If the teacher is dealing with the same language or topic, the students can still use the book to revise that particular language/vocabulary. But the same comments apply here as for omission. If too much of the textbook is replaced, both students and teacher may wonder if it is worth bothering with it at all.

The third option is to *add* to what is in the book. If the lesson is rather boring, too controlled, or if it gives no chance for students to use what they are learning in a personal kind of way, the teacher may want to add activities and exercises which extend the students' engagement with the language or topic.

Addition is a good alternative since it uses the textbook's

strengths but marries them with the teacher's own skills and perceptions of the class in front of him or her.

The final option is for the teacher to *adapt* what is in the book. If a reading text in the textbook is dealt with in a boring or uncreative way, if an invitation sequence is too predictable or if the teacher simply wants to deal with the material his or her way, he or she can adapt the lesson, using the same basic material, but doing it in his or her own style.

Using textbooks creatively is one of the premier teaching skills. However good the material is, most experienced teachers do not go through it word for word. Instead, they use the best bits, add to some exercises and adapt others. Sometimes, they replace textbook material with their own ideas – or ideas from other teachers and books – and occasionally they may omit the textbook lesson completely.

What do adding, adapting and replacing look like?

In the following four examples, we are going to show how textbook material can be used creatively by teachers.

Example 1: addition (intermediate)

Most textbooks have word lists, sometimes at the back of the book, sometimes at the end of a unit or a section. These are usually ignored, except by some students who often write inaccurate translations of the words. Teachers seldom touch them. Yet here is a chance to add to what the textbook provides in enjoyable and useful ways.

The following word list occurs after three lessons of intermediate material.

admire	exciting	killer	professor
attendance	experience	law	protection
attractive	factor	leader	record
bad	fair-haired	lovely	rugged
beautiful	fair-skinned	lover	scenic
boring	fantastic	magnificent	sick
cute	fascinating	Melanin	skin cancer
dangerous	flight	memorable	song
dark-haired	attendant	motorway	striking
dark-skinned	freckles	moving	stunning
die	gang	newscaster	sunburnt
doctor	good-looking	picturesque	suntanned
dramatic	handsome	pig	trust
elegant	impressive	place	Ultra violet
event	interesting	pretty	unmemorable
			victim

There are immediately things that we can do with such an apparently static piece of text. They fall into three categories: personal engagement, word formation, and word games.

Personal engagement: the teacher can ask students to discuss questions like 'Which words have a positive meaning? Which words have a negative meaning?' After they have discussed this with other students, they might come up with 'attractive' and 'magnificent' as positive words and 'dangerous' and 'sunburnt' as negative words. The teacher then asks the same question about the words in these phrases: 'dangerous game', 'dangerous lover', 'dramatic success', 'dramatic failure', 'expensive outfit', 'expensive train ticket' etc., to show how words change their connotation.

The teacher can ask students to list their five favourite words from the list – words that appeal to them because of their meaning, sound, spelling etc.

The teacher can ask whether any of the words look or sound like words in their language and whether they mean the same. This is especially useful for other Romance languages.

Finally, the teacher can ask students which words will be most useful to them in the future.

All of these questions ask the students to almost physically *Engage* with the meaning of the words – and what the words say to them. The word list has immediately become dynamic, not static.

Word study: the teacher can ask a number of questions about how the words are constructed. Students can be asked to make a list of words which are stressed on the first, second or third syllables. They can be asked how many of the adjectives can be changed into verbs and/or what endings the verbs would need if they were changed into adjectives. They can be asked to identify compound words (made up from two words – e.g. 'dark-skinned', 'skin cancer', 'suntanned') and say how they are formed.

There are many other possible activities here: how we make contrary meanings by adding 'un-' or 'in-' for example, how we give adjectives a comparative form, which of the verbs are 'regular' and what sound their past tense endings make etc. In each case, using a word list reminds students of some of the rules governing words and their grammar.

Word games: after a discussion about headlines, the students are asked to use words from the list in headlines for a bad tabloid newspaper, e.g. 'Attractive doctor in dramatic motorway experience!'

The word list can be used for 'expansion' too. The teacher gives the students a sentence like 'The man kissed the woman' and asks them to expand it using words from the list and adding any necessary grammar words too. They might produce something like 'The attractive fair-haired man with dramatic but elegant suntanned freckles kissed the fascinating pretty flight attendant in front of the dangerous woman on the motorway'.

There are many other game-like activities. Their purpose is to get students using and playing with the words in a word list – something often seen as dreary and uninteresting.

Example 2: adaptation (elementary/pre-intermediate)

In this example, the teacher decides that though there is absolutely nothing wrong with the textbook page in front of him, he wants to do it differently, perhaps for motivational reasons, perhaps just because he'll enjoy it more or because he thinks the students need the kind of role-play activity he is planning.

In the textbook he is using, the students are studying a unit called 'keeping the customer satisfied'. In the last class, they discussed whether they agreed that 'the customer is always right'. They studied words (like 'polite' and 'rude') with positive and negative meanings. They did a 'customer service' questionnaire about places they knew and they listened to people talking about good and bad service. In groups, they discussed whether staff needed different qualities in different places. The next page of the textbook is reproduced on page 115.

Instead of having students discuss the implications of the bank manager's decision to dress informally, the teacher tells them that they are going to write telephone dialogues for the following situation: an important customer has complained to the head office of 'The Old Trusted Bank' because his local bank manager was wearing jeans and a sweatshirt when the customer had a meeting with him or her the other day. Why did he do it? What's wrong with it? The personnel director from the head office rings up the bank manager to discuss the issue.

After students have written the dialogues, they read/act them out and the students are asked who they agree with: the head office or the manager?

In groups, they now role-play a head office meeting in which a committee decides whether to let staff dress informally or not. While they are doing this, the teacher goes around listening. If he hears that students use 'will', 'might' or 'won't' perfectly correctly, he moves on to the next section of the book. If students either don't use these verbs correctly (as he expects them not to) or if they hardly use them at all, he gets them to open the book and do exercises 1 to 3. He might then finish the sequence by having students write from the head office to the local bank manager telling him or her what they think about informal clothes and what they are going to do about it.

The teacher's use of role-play, letter-writing etc. is neither better nor worse than the material in the textbook: it is simply different because the teacher thought it would be more appropriate for a particular group of students and their teacher on a particular day.

The example shows how a teacher takes an original textbook idea, adapts it, putting in his own activities whilst staying faithful to the language and topic of the writers. He is perfectly happy to use the material (exercises 1-3) if necessary but simply wants to give the lesson his own 'spin'.

Example 3: replace (lower intermediate)

In this example of replacing textbook material with a teacher's own ideas, the teacher's decision to try and find his own material leads to a radically different type of lesson.

The textbook he is using wants students to practise the 'would like' construction in sentences like 'I'd like to live in a sunny country', 'She'd like to live on her own', 'They'd like to move to Kansas' etc. The material looks

A CHANGE OF IMAGE
will, may/might for prediction

1 Discuss these questions in groups.

1. Have you got a bank account? If so, what type is it?
2. Do you usually go to a bank for money or do you use cash machines?
3. How often do you take out money?

2 The man in the picture is a bank manager. He works in a very traditional bank in Scotland, but he has decided to change his image and wear casual clothes to work. Look at the possible consequences of his decision, and make sentences using *will*, *might* or *won't*.

Examples: *I think the bank will lose business.*
or *I think the bank may/might lose business.*
or *I don't think the bank will lose business.*
or *The bank won't (will not) lose business.*

CONSEQUENCES

Bank	Employees	Customers	Bank manager
lose business	start wearing casual clothes	be upset	get into trouble
get more young customers	think it's funny	complain	lose his job

Discuss your answers with a partner.

3 Can you add one more possible consequence to each category? Compare your answers in groups.

4 In your groups, choose one or two of the following situations and make a list of the possible consequences.

1. The Johnsons are a family of mother, father, sixteen-year-old son and two daughters, aged thirteen and eleven. One day the two daughters decide to become vegetarian. How will this affect the family?

104   Unit 16 KEEPING THE CUSTOMER SATISFIED

From *True to Life Pre-Intermediate* by Ruth Gairns and Stuart Redman

perfectly all right, but he fears that both he and his students will find it a bit boring. Instead, he decides to combine the structure practice with an idea he has had and wanted to use for some time.

At the beginning of the class, he asks students whether they like music and if so, what kind. Eventually (depending on the discussion), he tells them that they are going to listen to four different pieces/extracts and for each one, they should complete the following chart, working on their own.

	piece 1	piece 2	piece 3	piece 4
colour				
mood				
thermometer 0–100°				
Where would you like to hear it?				
Who would you like to hear it with?				

For the colour box, they should say what colour the music is (green, red, light blue etc.). They should then say what mood the music is (happy, sad, angry etc.) and what temperature it causes for their own personal thermometer (does it leave them cold or fire them up?)

When the teacher has played the four extracts, students compare their answers – probably in pairs first so that the teacher can then ask if anyone wants to tell the class about it. Finally, students can write a paragraph describing one of the pieces of music, e.g.

The extract from the Ebony Concerto was black and red to me. It was angry and funny at the same time and it made me quite excited. I'd like to hear it in a jazz club, I think, and I'd like to take my brother with me. I think it's his kind of music.

This kind of replacement activity, if used sparingly, is really good for the teacher and the class. It completely changes the atmosphere and its unusualness makes it memorable. The students practise the language the textbook wants them to, but in a completely different context.

In this particular case, a lot depends on the music you choose. The four extracts must be different one from the other, and they must be extracts which provoke strong reactions.

So why use textbooks at all? There are some teachers who have a very poor opinion of textbooks. They say they are boring, stifling (for both teacher and students) and often inappropriate for the class in front of them. Such people want to rely on their own ideas, snippets from reference books, pages from magazines, ideas from the students themselves and a variety of other sources.

Most teachers and students would recognise the truth behind these criticisms of textbooks – whether they teach language, mathematics, or geography. They are sometimes uninteresting and lacking in variety, for example, and all teachers can remember times when they saw the way a textbook treated a piece of language or a reading text and thought they could do it much better themselves. Added to this must be the ever-present danger that both teacher and students will get locked into the book, using its content as the only material which is taken into the classroom, always approaching a piece of teaching and learning in the way the book says it should be done. In such circumstances, the book becomes like a millstone around the necks of all concerned, removing, as it does, the very possibility of *Engagement* which its writer(s) hoped to provoke in the first place. As a result, some teachers take the decision to do without textbooks altogether, a decision which may well be of benefit to their students if, and only if, the teacher has the experience and time to provide a consistent programme of work on his or her own and if he or she has a bank of materials to back up the decisions that are taken. Such a decision will need the agreement of the students too.

For the vast majority of teachers who do use them, textbooks are just collections of material. However well they are planned, they can be inappropriate for teachers and students who should approach them with a degree of healthy scepticism which allows them not only to assess their contents carefully but also to use the textbooks judiciously for their own ends, rather than have the textbook use and control them.

Despite these worries about the dangers of textbook use, it should be pointed out that students often feel more positive about textbooks than some teachers. For them, the textbook is reassuring. It allows them to look forward and back, giving them a chance to prepare for what's coming and review what they have done. Now that books tend to be much more colourful than in the old days, students enjoy looking at the visual material in front of them.

For teachers too, textbooks have many advantages. In the first place, they have a consistent syllabus and vocabulary will have been chosen with care. Good textbooks have a range of reading and listening material and workbooks, for example, to back them up. They have dependable teaching sequences and, at the very least, they offer teachers something to fall back on when they run out of ideas of their own.

It is precisely because not everything in the textbook is wonderful – and because teachers want to bring their own personality to the teaching task – that addition, adaptation, and replacement are so important. That is when the teacher's own creativity really comes into play. That's when the dialogue between the teacher and the textbook really works for the benefit of the students.

w should teachers choose textbooks?

At many stages during their careers, teachers have to decide what books to use. How should they do this, and on what basis will they be able to say that one book is better or more appropriate than another?

There are nine main areas which teachers will want to consider in the books which they are looking at, as the table on page 119 shows (the issues are not in any significant order).

But when completing the questions from the table, teachers should try to follow this 4-stage procedure.

Analysis: the teacher can look through the various books on offer, analysing each for answers to the questions on the next page. It helps to have a chart to write down the answers for this so that the information is clearly displayed.

Piloting: by far the best way to find a book's strengths and weaknesses is to try it out with a class, seeing which lessons work and which don't. If teachers are teaching more than one group at the same level, they may want to teach two different books to compare them.

Consultation: before choosing a book, teachers should try and find out if any of their colleagues have used the book before and how well they got on with it. Through discussion, they can get an idea about whether or not the book is likely to be right for them.

Gathering opinions: anyone who might have an opinion on the book is worth speaking to, from the publisher and bookshop owners, to colleagues and friends. It is also a good idea to let students look through the book and see how they react to a first sight of it. If they express a preference which you agree with, they are likely to be more committed to the textbook.

Although choosing a textbook is an important step, it is what a teacher does with such a book once it has been selected that really matters.

area	questions to consider
1 price	How expensive is the textbook? Can the students afford it? Will they have to buy an accompanying workbook? Can they afford both? What about the teacher; can he or she pay for the teacher's book and tapes?
2 availability	Is the course available? Are all its components (students' book, teacher's book, workbook etc.) in the shops now? What about the next level (for the next term/semester)? Has it been published? Is it available? What about tapes, videos etc.?
3 layout and design	Is the book attractive? Does the teacher feel comfortable with it? Do the students like it? How user-friendly is the design? Does it get in the way of what the book is trying to do or does it enhance it?
4 methodology	What kind of teaching and learning does the book promote? Can teachers and students build appropriate *ESA* sequences from it? Is there a good balance between *Study* and *Activation*?
5 skills	Does the book cover the four skills (reading, writing, listening and speaking) adequately? Is there a decent balance between the skills? Are there opportunities for both *Study* and *Activation* in the skills work? Is the language of the reading and listening texts appropriate? Are the speaking and writing tasks likely to *Engage* the students' interest?
6 syllabus	Is the syllabus of the book appropriate for your students? Does it cover the language points you would expect? Are they in the right order? Do the reading and listening texts increase in difficulty as the book progresses?
7 topic	Does the book contain a variety of topics? Are they likely to engage the students' interest? Does the teacher respond to them well? Are they culturally appropriate for the students? Are they too adult or too childish?
8 stereotyping	Does the book represent people and situations in a fair and equal way? Are various categories of people treated equally? Is there stereotyping of certain nationalities? Does the book display conscious or unconscious racism or sexism?
9 teacher's guide	Is there a good teacher's guide? Is it easy to use? Does it have all the answers the teacher might need? Does it offer alternatives to lesson procedures? Does it contain a statement of intention which the teacher and students feel happy with?

Conclusions   In this chapter we have

* looked at four different options for textbook use when for some reason the teacher decides that (the lesson in) the textbook is not appropriate for the class: the options (according to Neville Grant) are *omit*, *replace*, *add* and *adapt*.
* said that textbook use is one of a teacher's main skills.
* looked at examples of adding to, adapting and replacing textbook material.
* discussed the criticisms often levelled at textbooks: that they are boring, inappropriate and lacking in variety, for example. But we have said that their advantages (clarity, solid progression, attractiveness) often outweigh these disadvantages, and that it is precisely because of some of their perceived defects that teachers need to use them creatively.
* asked how teachers should choose textbooks and identified nine areas which they need to consider: price, availability, layout and design, methodology, skills, syllabus, topic, stereotyping and the teacher's guide. We suggested that teachers should investigate these areas through analysis, piloting, consultation and the gathering of opinions from students and colleagues.

Looking ahead

* In the next chapter, *How to plan lessons*, we are going to look at how to decide what to teach for a particular class. Part of the planning will focus on the best way to use the textbook.
* The last chapter looks at problems some or all of which teachers encounter at various stages of their careers.

How to plan lessons

- Why plan at all?
- What are the aims of a plan?
- What should be in a plan?
- What questions do we need to ask?
- What form should a plan take?
- How should teachers plan a sequence of lessons?

Why plan at all?

Some teachers with experience seem to have an ability to think on their feet, which allows them to believe that they do not need to plan their lessons. However, most teachers go on preparing lessons throughout their careers, even if the plans are very informal.

For students, evidence of a plan shows them that the teacher has devoted time to thinking about the class. It strongly suggests a level of professionalism and a commitment to the kind of preparation they might reasonably expect. Lack of a plan may suggest the opposite of these teacher attributes.

For the teacher, a plan – however informal – gives the lesson a framework, an overall shape. It is true that he or she may end up departing from it at stages of the lesson, but at the very least it will be something to fall back on. Of course, good teachers are flexible and respond creatively to what happens in the classroom, but they also need to have thought ahead, have a destination they want their students to reach, and know how they are going to get there.

Planning helps, then, because it allows teachers to think about where they're going and gives them time to have ideas for tomorrow's and next week's lessons. In the classroom, a plan helps to remind teachers what they intended to do – especially if they get distracted or momentarily forget what they had intended. Finally, planning helps because it gives students confidence: they know immediately whether a teacher has thought about the lesson, and they respond positively to those that have.

No plan is written on tablets of stone, however. On the contrary, the plan is just that – a plan, possibilities for the lesson which may or may not come about, in other words. Of course, we will be happy if things go 'according to plan', but they often don't. As we said at the very beginning of this book (page 6), all sorts of things can go wrong: equipment not working, bored students, students who've 'done it before', students who need to ask unexpected questions or who want or need to pursue unexpected pathways etc. That's when the teacher has to be flexible, has to be able to leave the plan for however long it takes to satisfy the students' needs at that point in the lesson. Sometimes, the plan has to be abandoned completely and it is only after the lesson that the teacher can look at it again and see if some parts of it are recoverable for future lessons.

There is one particular situation in which planning is especially important, and that is when a teacher is to be observed as part of an assessment or performance review. The observer needs to have a clear idea of what the teacher intends in order to judge the success of the lesson.

What are the aims of a plan?

As we saw in Chapter 1, a good lesson needs to contain a judicious blend of coherence and variety. A good plan needs to reflect this.

Coherence means that students can see a logical pattern to the lesson. Even if there are three separate activities, for example, there has to be some connection between them – or at the very least a perceptible reason for changing direction. In this context, it would not make sense to have students listen to a tape, ask a few comprehension questions and then change the activity completely to something totally unrelated to the listening. And if the following activity only lasted for five minutes before something completely different was then attempted, we might well want to call the lesson incoherent.

Nevertheless, the effect of having a class do a 45-minute drill would be equally damaging. The lack of variety coupled with the relentlessness of such a procedure would militate against the possibility of real student engagement. However present it might be at the beginning of the session, it would be unlikely to be sustained. There has to be some variety in a lesson period.

The ideal compromise is to plan a lesson that has an internal coherence but which nevertheless allows students to do different things.

What should be in a plan?

The kind of plan that teachers make for themselves can be as scrappy or as detailed as the teacher feels is necessary. If you look at experienced teachers' notebooks, you may find that they have simply written down the name of an activity, a page number from a book, the opening of a dictation activity or notes about a particular student. Such notes look rather empty, but may, in fact, give the teacher all she needs to remind her of all the necessary elements. Other teachers, however, put in much more detail, writing in what they're going to do together with notes like 'remember to collect homework'.

On teacher training courses, trainers often ask for a written plan which follows a particular format. The formats will vary depending on the trainer and the course, but all plans have the same ingredients. They say who is going to be taught, what they are going to learn or be taught, how they are going to learn or be taught, and with what.

The first thing such a written plan needs to detail is who the students are: How many are there in the class? What ages? What sexes? What are they like? Cooperative? Quiet? Difficult to control? Experienced teachers have all this information in their heads when they plan; teachers in training will be expected to write it down.

The next thing the plan has to contain is what the teachers/students want to do: study a piece of grammar, write a narrative, listen to an interview, read a passage etc. Looking through a plan, an objective observer should be able to discern a logical sequence of things to be studied and/or activated.

The third aspect of a plan will say how the teacher/students is/are going to do it. Will they work in pairs? Will the teacher just put on a tape or will the class start by discussing dangerous sports for example (see the Eddie Edwards tapescript on page 107)? Once again, an objective reader of the plan should be able to identify a logical sequence of classroom events. If four activities in a row are teacher-led dictations, we might start to think that the sequence is highly repetitive and that, as a result, the students are likely to get very demotivated by this incessant repetition. For each activity, the teacher will usually indicate how long she expects it to take and what classroom materials or aids she is going to use. The plan will say what is going to be used for the activities: A tape recorder? Photocopies? An overhead projector?

Lastly, the plan will talk about what might go wrong (and how it can be dealt with) and how the lesson fits in with lessons before and after it.

In order to be able to say these things, however, we need to go a little bit deeper and ask some searching questions about the activities we intend to use.

What questions do we need to ask?

For each activity we intend to use in the lesson (whether it's a role-play about building supermarkets or a writing activity while listening to music), we need to be able to answer a number of questions in our own minds. They are:

Who exactly are the students for this activity? As we said above, the make-up of the class will influence the way teachers plan. Their age, level, cultural background and individual characteristics have to be taken into account when deciding to use an activity. Teachers often have a section called *Description of the class* in their plans to remind themselves and/or show an observer what they know about their students.

Why do you want to do it? There has to be a good reason for taking an activity into a classroom apart from the fact that the teacher happens to like it or because it looks interesting.

What will it achieve? It is vitally important to have thought about what an activity will achieve. How will students have changed as a result of it? It might give the students a greater understanding of an area of vocabulary. It might give them greater fluency in one particular topic area, or it might have the effect of providing students with better strategies for coping with long and difficult stories told orally, for example. It might achieve a change of atmosphere in the class, too. If it is difficult to say what an activity might achieve, then it may well be that the activity is not worth using. In a plan, this is often called *Aims* and most trainers expect the aims to be quite specific. 'Writing' is too general an aim for observers to get much of an idea of what the teacher wants to do, whereas 'to train students to use appropriate paragraph construction' does describe exactly what the teacher intends.

How long will it take? Some activities which sound very imaginative end up lasting for only a very short time. Others demand setting-up time, discussion time, student-planning time etc. One of the things that undermines the students' confidence in the teacher is if they never finish what they set out to do. One of the things that irritates them most is when teachers run on after the bell has gone because they have to finish an activity. Thinking about how long an activity will take is a vital part of planning. Most teachers indicate the intended *Timing* of an activity in their plan.

What might go wrong? If teachers try and identify problems that might arise in the lesson, they are in a much better position to deal with them if and when they occur. The attempt to identify problems will also give the teacher insight into the language and/or the activity which is to be used. Teachers often call this *Anticipated problems* in their plan.

What will be needed? Teachers have to decide whether they are going to use the board or the tape recorder, an overhead projector or some role cards. It is also important to consider the limitations of the classroom and the equipment. In their plans, teachers usually indicate the *Teaching aids* they are going to use or attach copies of print material the students are going to work with.

How does it work? If teachers wanted to use the poetry activity on page 76, how would they actually do it? Who does what first? How and when should students be put in pairs or groups? When does the teacher give instructions? What are those instructions? Experienced teachers may have procedures firmly fixed in their minds but even they, when they try something new, need to think carefully about the mechanics of the activity. Teachers often call this *Procedure* in their plans and indicate what kind of activity it is, sometimes in note form. For example, 'TQ $\longrightarrow$ SA' means stages where the teacher leads a question and answer session with the students, and 'S $\longrightarrow$ S' means pairwork.

How will it fit in with what comes before and after it? An activity on its own may be useful, engaging and full of good language. But what connection, if any, does it have to the activities which come before and after it? Is there a language tie-in? Perhaps two or three activities are linked by topic, one leading into the other. Perhaps an activity has no connection with the one before it: it is there to break up any monotony in a lesson or to act as a 'gear change'. The point of answering this question for ourselves is to ensure that we have some reasonable vision of the overall shape for our lesson and that it is not composed of unrelated scraps.

What form should a plan take?	There is no 'correct' format for a lesson plan. The most important thing about it is that it should be useful for the teacher and for anyone who is observing him or her. Some teachers, for example, might write their plan on cards. Others will prefer handwritten sheets from a notepad, others will type it out immaculately on a word processor.

Some teachers highlight parts of their plan with coloured pens. Some divide their plans into columns with timings on the left, procedures in the middle and comments in a right-hand column. Still others have an 'introduction' page with facts about the class and the aims of the lesson before going into detail.

Some teachers write down exactly what they are going to say and note down each sentence that the students are going to say. Other teachers use note-form hints to themselves (e.g. 'T checks comprehension') or just write 'pairwork' or 'solowork' or 'whole class', for example.

When teachers are in training, it will be sensible to take the trainer's preferences into account. Practising teachers should experiment with plan formats until they find one that is most useful for them. By looking at the plan in the Task File on page 171 with its strengths and weaknesses, it will be possible to come to some conclusions about how to design your own.

How should teachers plan a sequence of lessons?	In Chapter 1, we discussed the need for variety in classroom activities and teacher behaviour as an antidote to student (and teacher) boredom. This means that, when teachers plan a lesson, they build in changes of activity and a variety of exercises. It may well be that the lesson has an overall theme, but within that theme the students do different things. This was demonstrated by our classroom sequences in Chapter 4 and Chapters 6–10. What was being sought for in each case was a confidence-inspiring coherence lit up by variety and interest.

The same principles apply to a sequence of lessons stretching, for example, over two weeks or a month. Once again, students will want to see a coherent pattern of progress and topic-linking so that there is a connection between lessons and so that they can perceive some overall aims and objectives. Most find this preferable to a series of 'one-off' lessons.

However, two dangers may prejudice the success of a sequence of lessons. The first is predictability and the second is sameness. Despite the need for coherence, teachers must remember that if students know exactly what to expect they are likely to be less motivated than if their curiosity is aroused. In the same way, they may feel less enthusiastic about today's lesson if it starts with exactly the same kind of activity as yesterday's lesson.

An ideal two-week sequence has threads running through it which are based on a topic or topics. During the two weeks, all four skills will be covered appropriately. During the two weeks, the language being taught will happen in a logical sequence. Most importantly of all, there will be a range of activities which bring variety and interest to the learning process.

Perhaps the most important thing to remember, however, is that a long teaching sequence (e.g. two weeks) is made up of shorter sequences (e.g. six lessons) which are themselves made up of smaller sequences (one or two per lesson perhaps). And at the level of a teaching sequence we have to ensure the presence of our three elements, *Engage*, *Study* and *Activate*.

Conclusions

In this chapter we have
- discussed the purpose of planning: it helps to focus our minds, it helps to have something to refer to in the middle of the class, it shows students that we are professional and that we care.
- said that, whatever the format of a plan, it should tell us who is going to learn or be taught, what they are going to learn or be taught, how they are going to do it and what with.
- asked a number of important questions which teachers need to consider before they start to plan an activity: Why do you want to do it? What will it achieve? How long will it take? What might go wrong? What will you need to do it? How will it fit in with what comes before and after it?
- introduced the terms 'description of the class, aims, timing, anticipated problems, teaching aids, procedures' as headings which some teachers use to organise their plans.
- suggested that the actual format of a lesson plan is very much a matter of personal preference, but that trainers may want to guide trainees into certain formats.

Looking ahead

- In the next and final chapter of this book, we will turn our attention to the 'what ifs?' of teaching – problems that frequently crop up – and how to solve them.

What if?

- What if students are all at different levels?
- What if the class is very big?
- What if students keep using their own language?
- What if students are uncooperative?
- What if students don't want to talk?
- What if students don't understand the listening tape?
- What if some students-in-groups finish before everybody else?

What if students are all at different levels?

One of the biggest problems teachers face is a lesson where the students are at different levels – some with quite competent English, some whose English isn't very good, and some whose English is only just getting started. As with many other classroom subjects, teachers face this problem every day unless the most rigorous selection has taken place. What then are the possible ways of dealing with the situation?

Use different materials: when teachers know who the good and less good students are, they can form different groups. While one group is working on a piece of language study (e.g. the past continuous), the other group might be reading a story or doing a more advanced grammar exercise. Later, while the better group or groups are discussing a topic, the weaker group or groups might be doing a parallel writing exercise, or sitting round a tape recorder listening to a tape.

In schools where there are self-study facilities (a study centre, or separate rooms), the teacher can send one group of students off to work there in order to concentrate on another. Provided the self-study task is purposeful, the students who go out of the classroom will not feel cheated.

If the self-study area is big enough, of course, it is an ideal place for different-level learning. While one group is working on a grammar activity in one corner, two other students can be listening to a tape and another group again will be consulting an encyclopedia while a different set of colleagues is working at a computer screen.

Do different tasks with the same material: where teachers use the same material with the whole class, they can encourage students to do different tasks depending on their abilities. A reading text can have questions at three different levels, for example. The teacher tells the students to see how far they can get: the better ones will quickly finish the first two and have to work hard on the third. The weakest students may not get past the first task.

In a language study exercise, the teacher can ask for simple repetition from some students, but ask others to use the new language in more complex sentences. If the teacher is getting students to give answers or opinions, she can make it clear that one word will do for some students whereas longer and more complex contributions are expected from others. Lastly, in role-plays and other speaking or group activities, she can ensure that students have roles or functions which are appropriate to their level.

Ignore the problem: it is perfectly feasible to hold the belief that, within a heterogeneous group, students will find their own level. In speaking and writing activities, for example, the better students will probably be more daring, in reading and listening, they will understand more completely and more quickly. However, the danger of this position is that students will either be bored by the slowness of their colleagues or frustrated by their inability to keep up.

Use the students: some teachers adopt a strategy of peer help and teaching so that better students can help weaker ones. They can work with them in pairs or groups, explaining things, or providing good models of language performance in speaking and writing. Thus, when teachers put students in groups, they can ensure that weak and strong students are put together. However, this has to be done with great sensitivity so that students don't get alienated by their over-knowledgeable peers or oppressed by their obligatory teaching role.

Many teachers, faced with students at different levels, adopt a mixture of solutions like the ones we have suggested here.

What if the class is very big?

In big classes, it is difficult for the teacher to make contact with the students at the back and it is difficult for the students to ask for and receive individual attention. It may seem impossible to organise dynamic and creative teaching and learning sessions. Frequently, big classes mean that it is not easy to have students walking around or changing pairs etc. Most importantly, big classes can be quite intimidating for inexperienced teachers.

Despite the problems of big classes, there are things which teachers can do.

Use worksheets: one solution is for teachers to hand out worksheets for many of the tasks which they would normally do with the whole class – if the class was smaller. When the feedback stage is reached, teachers can go through the worksheets with the whole group – and all the students will get the benefit.

Use pairwork and groupwork: in large classes, pairwork and groupwork play an important part since they maximise student participation. Even where chairs and desks cannot be moved, there are ways of doing this: first rows turn to face second rows, third rows to face fourth rows etc.

When using pairwork and groupwork with large groups, it is important to make instructions especially clear, to agree how to stop the activity (many teachers just raise their hands until students notice them and gradually quieten down) and to give good feedback.

Use chorus reaction: since it becomes difficult to use a lot of individual repetition and controlled practice in a big group, it may be more appropriate to use students in chorus. The class can be divided into two halves – the front five rows and the back five rows, for example, or the left-hand and right-hand sides of the classroom. Each row/half can then speak a part in a dialogue, ask or answer a question, repeat sentences or words. This is especially useful at lower levels.

Use group leaders: teachers can enlist the help of a few group leaders. They can be used to hand out copies, check that everyone in their group (or row or half) has understood a task, collect work and give feedback.

Think about vision and acoustics: big classes often are (but not always) in big rooms. Teachers have to make sure that what they show or write can be seen and that what they say or play to the whole group can be heard.

Use the size of the group to your advantage: big groups have disadvantages of course, but they also have one main advantage – they are bigger, so that humour, for example, is funnier, drama is more dramatic, a good class feeling is warmer and more enveloping. Experienced teachers use this potential to organise exciting and involving classes.

No-one chooses to have a large group: it makes the job of teaching even more challenging than it already is. However, teachers do find themselves, in various teaching situations around the world, dealing with groups of thirty, or fifty, or even sometimes above and beyond a hundred students. Some of the suggestions above will help to turn a potential disaster into some kind of a success.

What if students keep using their own language? One of the problems that teachers sometimes face with students who all share the same native language is that they use their native language rather than English to perform classroom tasks. This may be because they want to communicate something important, and so they use language in the best way they know! They will almost certainly find speaking in their language a lot easier than struggling with English.

But, however much teachers might sympathise with their students, the need to have them practising English (rather than their own language) remains paramount.

There are a number of things that can be done in this situation.

Talk to them about the issues: teachers can discuss with students how

129

they should all feel about using English and/or their own language in the class. Teachers should try to get their students' agreement that overuse of their own language means that they will have less chance to learn English; that using their own language during speaking activities denies them chances for rehearsal and feedback.

Encourage them to use English appropriately: teachers should make it clear that there is not a total ban on their own language – it depends on what's happening. In other words, a little bit of the students' native language when they're working on a reading text is not too much of a problem, but a speaking *Activate* exercise will lose its purpose if not done in English.

Only respond to English use: teachers can make it clear by their behaviour that they want to hear English. They can ignore what students say in their own language.

Create an English environment: teachers themselves should speak English for the majority of the time, so that, together with the use of listening material and video, the students are constantly exposed to how English sounds, and what it feels like. Some teachers anglicise their students' names too.

Keep reminding them: teachers should be prepared to go round the class during a speaking exercise encouraging, cajoling, even pleading with them to use English – and offering help if necessary. This technique, often repeated, will gradually change most students' behaviour over a period of time.

What if students are uncooperative?

All experienced teachers will remember students they have not enjoyed working with, and most teachers can recall times when students were deliberately uncooperative, sometimes to a point of great discomfort for the teacher.

Lack of cooperation can take many forms: constant chattering in class, not listening to the teacher, failure to do any homework, blunt refusal to do certain activities, constant lateness and even rudeness. Sometimes, things get so bad that students complain to someone in authority.

There are a number of things teachers can do to try and solve the problems of uncooperative classes.

Talk to individuals: teachers can speak to individual members of the class outside the classroom. They can ask them what they feel about the class, why there's a problem and what they think can be done about it.

Write to individuals: the same effect can be achieved simultaneously with all students by writing them a (confidential) letter. In the letter, the teacher says that she thinks there's a serious problem in the class and that she wants to know what can be done about it. Students can be invited to write back in complete confidence. The replies which are received (and not all students will reply) will show what some of the problems are.

The only disadvantage to having students write to the teacher individually is that the teacher then has to write back to each of them!

Use activities: teachers can make it clear that some of the more enjoyable activities which students like to do will only be used when the class is functioning properly. Otherwise, they will be forced to fall back on more formal teaching and language study.

Enlist help: teachers should not have to suffer on their own! They should talk to colleagues and, if possible, get a friend to come and observe the class to see if they notice things that the teacher himself or herself is not aware of.

Make a language-learning contract: teachers can talk directly to the students about issues of teaching and learning. They can get the students' agreement to ways of behaving and find out what they expect or need from the teacher. This is the forming of a language-learning 'contract' and subjects covered can include such things as when the students should not use their language, what teachers expect from homework, arriving on time etc. But teachers will have to bind themselves to good teacher behaviour too.

When the contract is concluded, it forms a behaviour blueprint for everyone, and if students have said that they don't want people to talk in class all the time, for example, then they are likely to ensure that it doesn't happen often.

What if students don't want to talk?

Many teachers have come across students who don't seem to want to talk in class. Sometimes, this may have to do with the students' own characters. Sometimes, it is because there are other students who dominate and almost intimidate. Sometimes, it is because students are simply not used to talking freely – for reasons of culture and background. Perhaps, in their culture, women are traditionally expected to remain quiet in a mixed-sex group. Perhaps their culture finds in modesty a positive virtue. Perhaps they suffer from a fear of making mistakes and therefore 'losing face' in front of the teacher and their peers.

Whatever the reason, it makes no sense to try and bully such students into talking. It will probably only make them more reluctant to speak. There are other much better things to try.

Use pairwork: pairwork (and groupwork) will help to provoke quiet students into talking. When they are with one or perhaps two or three other students, they are not under so much pressure as they are if asked to speak in front of the whole class.

Allow them to speak in a controlled way at first: asking quiet students for instant fluency may be doomed to failure, initially. It is better to do it in stages, as in the following example. The teacher can dictate sentences which the students only have to fill in parts of before reading them out.

Thus, the teacher dictates 'One of the most beautiful things I have ever seen is ...' and the students have to complete it for themselves. They then read out their sentences, e.g. 'One of the most beautiful things I have ever seen is Mount Fuji at sunset' etc.

In general, it may be a good idea to let students write down what they are going to say before they say it. Reading sentences aloud does not demand the kind of risk-taking fluency which spontaneous conversation does. But once students have read out their sentences, the teacher or other students can ask them questions. Psychologically, they are more likely to be able to respond.

Use 'acting out' and reading aloud: getting students to act out dialogues is one way of encouraging quiet students. However, acting out does not just mean reading aloud. The teacher has to work with the students like a drama coach, working out when the voice should rise and fall, where the emphasis goes, what emotion the actor should try to convey. When the student then acts out the role, the teacher can be confident that it will sound good.

Use role-play: many teachers have found that quiet students speak more freely when they are playing a role – when they are not having to be themselves, in other words. As in our example on page 92, the use of role cards allows students to take on a new identity, one in which they can behave in uncharacteristic ways. It can be very liberating.

Use the tape recorder: if teachers have time, they can tell students to record what they would like to say, outside the lesson. The teacher then listens to the tape and points out possible errors. The student now has a chance to produce a more correct version when the lesson comes round, thus avoiding the embarrassment (for them) of making mistakes.

In Chapter 2, we said that a good student shows a willingness to experiment, to 'have a go'. Some students, however, feel inhibited about this, especially where speaking is concerned. The activities above are ways of getting them to change.

What if students don't understand the listening tape?

Sometimes, despite the teacher's best judgement – or the judgement of a textbook writer – listening material on tape seems to be too difficult for students to understand. However many times the teacher plays the tape (and after the third or fourth listening, the teacher and the students will be getting fairly desperate), it just doesn't work. The teacher abandons the activity and a general depression ensues.

There are a number of alternatives to this scenario which might help.

Introduce interview questions: if students find (or will find) an interview difficult, they can be given the questions first and encouraged to role-play the interview before listening to it. This will have great predictive power.

Use 'jigsaw listening': different groups can be given different taped excerpts (either on tape or – for some of them – as tapescripts). When the groups hear about each others' extracts, they can get the whole picture by putting the 'jigsaw' pieces together.

One task only: students can be given a straightforward task which does not demand too much detailed understanding. A useful possibility is to get them to describe the speaker on the tape – the sound of the voice will suggest sex, age, status etc.

Play a/the first segment only: instead of playing the whole tape, teachers can just play the first segment and then let students predict what's coming next. Our third example in Chapter 10 (see pages 104-6) was a version of this.

Use the tapescript (1): it can be cut into bits. The students put them in the right order as they listen.

Use the tapescript (2): the students can look at the tapescript of the first segment to give them confidence and ensure that they know what the tape is about.

Use the tapescript (3): students can read the tapescript before, during and after they listen. The tapescript can also have words or phrases blanked out.

Use vocabulary prediction: students can be given 'key' vocabulary before they listen again. They can then be asked to predict what the tape will be about and, because they now know some of the words, they may well understand more.

What if some students-in-groups finish before everybody else?

When teachers put students in groups and ask them to complete a task – designing a poster, discussing a reading text etc. – they can be sure that some groups will finish before others. If the activity has a competitive element (for example, who can solve a problem first), this is not a worry. But where no such element is present, the teacher is put in a quandary: should he stop the activity (which means not letting some finish) or let the others finish (which means boring the people who finished first)?

As in so many other cases, common sense has to prevail here. If only one group finishes way before the others, the teacher can work with that group or provide them with some 'spare activity' material. If only one group is left without having finished, the teacher may decide to stop the activity anyway – because the rest of the class shouldn't be kept waiting.

One way of dealing with the problem is for the teacher to carry around a selection of 'spare activities' – little worksheets, puzzles, readings etc. – which can be done quickly (in just a few minutes) and which will keep the early-finishing students happy until the others have caught up. Another solution is to plan extensions to the original task so that, if groups finish early, they can do extra work on it.

Conclusions   In this chapter we have

- talked about the problem of teaching mixed ability classes, suggesting either different material, different tasks, ignoring the problem or using students as ways of dealing with it.
- discussed the issue of large classes, suggesting ways of coping with them such as using worksheets, using pairwork and groupwork, using chorus reaction, using group leaders, thinking about vision and acoustics, and using the size of the group to your advantage.
- looked at solutions to the problem of students using their own language when we want them to be using English. We suggested talking to students about the issue, encouraging them to use English appropriately, only responding to English use, creating an English environment and continuing to remind them of the issue.
- studied the issue of uncooperative students, suggesting that where there is trouble we can talk to individuals, write to individuals, use activities, enlist help and get agreement on a language-learning contract.
- faced the problem of students who are reluctant to speak. Possible solutions included using pairwork, allowing students to speak in a controlled way first, using acting out and reading aloud, and using role-play.
- worried about situations where students are having real trouble with listening material. Among many alternatives, we can give them interview questions before they listen (again), give them different bits of the tape 'jigsaw', concentrate on one simple listening task only, only play the (first) bit of the tape, use the tapescript in a variety of ways and, finally, get students to predict listening content by giving them key vocabulary.
- suggested that teachers should always have some spare activities 'up their sleeve' for situations where some groups finish long before others.

How to Teach English
Task File

The material in this section can be photocopied for use in limited circumstances. Please see the notice on the back of the title page for the restrictions on photocopying.

Task File
Introduction

- The exercises in this section all relate to topics which are discussed in the chapter to which the exercises refer. Some expect definite answers while others ask only for the reader's opinions.
- These tasks are a mixture of *general* and/or *specific* exercises.

General exercises are those for which no specialised knowledge is required, e.g.

A Why is it difficult to describe a good learner? [page 7]

1 Think of two successful learners you know (excluding yourself). What positive qualities did/do they share?

2 What do you think it takes to be a good student in the following areas?

art boxing driving mathematics medicine swimming the violin

How many qualities apply to all the disciplines?

Specific exercises are those which ask readers to interact with the technical aspects of teaching which are being discussed, e.g.

D What teaching models have influenced current teaching practice? [page 30]

Answer these questions after reading the chapter.

a What do the following initials stand for?
   1 CLT   2 PPP   3 TBL
b What connection do the models in (a) have with the following?
   1 Straight Arrows lessons
   2 Boomerang lessons
   3 Patchwork lessons

- Not all tasks are so clearly general or specific. Much will depend on the reader and what knowledge he or she brings to the task.
- Tutors will, of course, decide when (and if) it is appropriate to use the tasks in this section. Readers on their own can look at the tasks at any stage, but where they are clearly more specific they may want to leave them until they have read the relevant (section of the) chapter in the book.

Chapter 1
How to be a good teacher

A What makes a good teacher? [page 1]

1 Think of two good teachers from your past. What personal qualities do/did they share?

2 Rate the following teacher qualities in order of importance (1-8).

❑ *They are good-looking.*　❑ *They are very entertaining.*
❑ *They can control the class*　❑ *They give interesting classes.*
❑ *They know their students.*　❑ *They can keep control.*
❑ *They prepare well.*　❑ *They know their subject.*

B How should teachers talk to students? [page 3]

1 You want to tell a low-level class about what you did last weekend. Write down the kind of language you might use.

2 Rate the following statements 0 (= totally disagree) to 5 (= totally agree).

a Teachers should speak very slowly and clearly to their foreign-language students. ❑

b Teachers should always use well-constructed sentences when they speak to their students. ❑

c Teachers should speak to their students like parents talk to their young children. ❑

d Teachers should speak normally to their students – as if they were talking to their own friends. ❑

e Teachers should only say things to students which the students will understand totally. ❑

C How should teachers give instructions? [page 4]

1 Put a tick (√) in the boxes if you think the instructions are good.

❑ Teacher: *Now I want you to work in pairs ... yes* (gesturing) *... that's right ... you two ... you two ... you two. Good. Now listen carefully. I want you to read this text* (holding up the book and pointing to it) *on page 26 and answer the questions ... OK? Now then, Ilona, what's the page? ... Good ... What are you going to do, Danuta ... ?*

❑ Teacher: *OK, this is the deal – and I hope you really enjoy this 'cos I spent a lot of time planning it, you know, in the flat when I should have been watching sport on my new Flatpic 2 TV – great programme –*

anyway, where was I, yes, well, because I'm ideologically committed to cooperative work, I thought you could probably access this grammar problem yourselves, by looking it up in your book in groups. OK?

☐ Teacher: (sitting at desk, looking at his/her notes). *Open your books on page 26. What's the answer to question 1?*

☐ Teacher: (holding up large picture): *Right, we're going to do something a bit different now. Fumiko ... everybody ... are you listening? Good. Right. Now ask me questions about the picture* (pointing to the picture, gesturing) *... questions with 'what' ... Anybody? Yes, Fumiko?*

2 What information would you have to get over if you wanted to explain how to

   a change a tyre?   b use a cash machine?   c fry an egg?

   Write the instructions you would give to a low-level group of students for one of these procedures.

D Who should talk in class? [page 4]

1 In a class of twenty students and one teacher how much speaking time will each student have in a 50-minute class (if they are working all together)?

2 Make a list of advantages and disadvantages of the teacher talking in an English class.

E What are the best kinds of lesson? [page 5]

1 Complete the following sentences about you.

   a When I was at school, the best lessons were ... .
   b The best lesson I have ever observed was ... .
   c I think the best kind of lessons that I can give are ... .

2 Give the following statements a score of 0 (= I disagree) to 5 (= I totally agree).

   a Good teachers keep students guessing about what they are going to do next. ☐
   b Teachers should be predictable, not anarchic. ☐
   c The worst kind of teacher is the one who does the same thing every class. ☐
   d Good teachers always look smart. ☐
   e Good teachers are always interesting. ☐

F How important is it to follow a pre-arranged plan? [page 5]

Re-write the following paragraph so that it reflects your own opinions.

Good teachers plan their classes minutely so that everything they do is pre-arranged. Once they are in the classroom, they follow their plan without deviation, always watching out for irrelevancies which the students may bring up and which would disrupt the plan.

Chapter 2
How to be a good learner

A   **Why is it difficult to describe a good learner? [page 7]**

1   Think of two successful learners you know (excluding yourself). What positive qualities did/do they share?

2   What do you think it takes to be a good student in the following areas?

art   boxing   driving   mathematics   medicine   swimming   the violin

How many qualities apply to all the disciplines?

B   **How important is the students' motivation? [page 8]**

1   Re-write these sentences so that they reflect your own opinion.

a It is very difficult for teachers to motivate students who are not interested in their subject.
b Teachers do not have to worry about the continuing motivation of students who are already motivated.
c You can only learn a language successfully if you love the culture of the language.
d I am interested in learning a foreign language because I want a job.

2   Think of a group of students. What would be motivating and de-motivating in the following areas?

activity   linguistic content   teacher's behaviour   topic   teacher's attitude

C   **Who is responsible for learning? [page 9]**

1   List the things you would put in a self-study centre for students if you had unlimited money. What would each item be designed to do?

2   Look at the following activities for students. What are they designed to do? How well do you think they achieve their aim?

a When you come across a word you don't know in a reading text do you
    • look the word up in a dictionary straightaway?
    • try and guess the meaning of the word and keep reading?
    • underline words you don't understand as you go along and ask the teacher later?

b List your ten favourite new words from units 20–25.

Which do you think is the best approach?

D   **What characteristics do good classroom learners share?
[page 10]**

1   Are you a good learner? List your own positive characteristics and the
ones which you think make you less successful.

2   Rate the following learner qualities in order of importance from
1 (= most important) to 10 (= least important).

❑ *getting to class on time*
❑ *liking English*
❑ *being careful about physical appearance*
❑ *asking questions*
❑ *having a go at every opportunity*
❑ *reflecting on how individual learning takes place*
❑ *doing homework*
❑ *looking for examples of English outside the classroom*
❑ *learning how to use dictionaries and grammar books*
❑ *getting enough sleep*

What other qualities would you add?

E   **What's special about teaching adults? [page 10]**

1   Make an advantages/disadvantages grid for children, adolescents and
adults.

2   Who do you think is being described in the examples? Put **C** = Children,
A = Adolescents, **Ad** = Adults or **?** = Don't know in the boxes.

❑ *A small group of students come to see you and say that they're finding
learning English much more difficult than they had hoped. They want to
stop the classes.*
❑ *After a lesson, a group of students come to see you and say 'We don't like
the way you're teaching. We want more grammar'.*
❑ *One of the students' favourite activities is the chanting of rhythmic
sentences to emphasise good pronunciation.*
❑ *Students get really excited when you offer to let them sing a song.*
❑ *Students play tricks such as hiding under desks and giving the wrong
names when you are taking the register.*
❑ *When you arrive late for class, some of the students are quietly getting on
with their work.*
❑ *When you ask a student to come out to the front of the class to take part
in a demonstration, he is extremely reluctant to do so because he is so
nervous.*
❑ *You get students in groups to play a board game adapted from a general
knowledge quiz. They are reluctant to play the game.*
❑ *You get students to write poems on the subject of friendship and you are
surprised and moved by their work.*

F   **What are the different levels? [page 12]**

1   Look at these descriptions of student competence. What level is being
described in each case, do you think?

<u>lower intermediate</u>
.... *Is beginning to be able to use English for basic
everyday needs.*

.... *Knows or remembers a few words or phrases.
Can even string together a very basic question
or sentence.*

.... *Knows virtually no English.*

.... *Uses a limited range of language, sufficient for
basic everyday practical needs.*

.... *Uses a wide range of language (with some
confidence) in all but the most demanding
situations.*

.... *Uses a moderate rate of language, sufficient for
most practical needs and personal
conversations.*

.... *Uses a very narrow range of English.*

(Adapted from the Bell English Language Learning Scale, Bell Language
Schools)

2   What three differences can you think of between

a a beginner and an advanced student?
b an elementary student and an upper-intermediate student?
c a beginner and a false beginner?
d a false beginner and an intermediate student?

G   **How should we teach the different levels? [page 13]**

What level are these activities appropriate for? Put **B** = Beginner,
I = Intermediate or **A** = Advanced in the boxes. Some may be
appropriate at more than one level.

☐ *Students write and assemble the front page of an imaginary newspaper
with stories you have given them and others they make up.*
☐ *Students listen to a dialogue between a railway official and a tourist
asking for information.*
☐ *Students listen to an interview with an actor talking about how she got
started.*
☐ *Students practise introducing themselves with language such as 'Pleased
to meet you', 'Hello, my name's Karen'.*
☐ *Students practise repeating/saying words with the /æ/ sound, e.g. c<u>a</u>b,
s<u>a</u>nd, b<u>a</u>t, <u>a</u>nd, <u>a</u>t etc.*
☐ *Students put together a radio commercial for a new kind of shoe.*
☐ *Students report back on an unsimplified work of English-language fiction.*
☐ *Students role-play choosing a dress in a clothes store.*
☐ *Students watch a video of a documentary about global warming.*

Chapter 3
How to manage teaching and learning

A **How should teachers use their physical presence in class? [page 15]**

How should teachers use their voices in class? [page 16]

1   Give a rating of 1 (= just right) to 5 (= absolutely terrible) for a teacher you remember well.

   ❑ *appearance*
   ❑ *audibility*
   ❑ *clarity*
   ❑ *general presence in class*
   ❑ *movement in class*
   ❑ *vocal quality*

   In the case of a low score, explain your reasons.
   Now score yourself as you are or are likely to be.

2   Try to complete this chart with situations/activities which might be appropriate for the behaviour described. If you cannot put anything in the column, explain why not.

teacher behaviour	appropriate situations
the teacher shouts	
the teacher is at the back of the class	
the teacher is at the front of the class	
the teacher is 'sitting' on a table round which four students are working	
the teacher is sitting on the floor	

B   How should teachers mark the stages of a lesson? [page 17]

1   Using your memory, experience and imagination, think of

   a three good ways of starting any lesson.
   b three good ways of ending any lesson.

2   Number the following ways of regaining the initiative in a noisy class in
order of personal preference and give your opinion of their
effectiveness (1 = most effective, 7 = least effective).

   a The teacher blows a whistle. ❏
   b The teacher claps his or her hands. ❏
   *c The teacher raises his or her hand, expecting students to raise their
      hands and quieten down.* ❏
   d The teacher shouts at students to be quiet. ❏
   e The teacher stands on a table and shouts at students to be quiet. ❏
   *f The teacher speaks quietly in the hope that students will quieten down
      to listen.* ❏
   *g The teacher stands in front of the class with arms folded, fixing the
      students with a baleful stare. The teacher waits.* ❏

C   What's the best seating arrangement for a class? [page 18]

1   Do you agree or disagree with the following statements? Give your
reasons.

   a Classes where students sit in straight rows are easier to control.
   *b Classes where students sit in straight rows are old-fashioned and stop
      people learning.*
   c Having students in straight rows is the best way to teach a large class.
   d It is important for students to face the teacher.
   e Students participate more fully in a class where students sit in straight rows.
   f Students understand things better when they sit in straight rows.

2   What do you think is the best seating arrangement for the following
situations? Explain your reasons.

   a You want to have a game in teams with a class of forty students.
   b In your class of fifteen students you want them to discuss a topic with you.
   c In your class of thirty students you want them to work in pairs.
   d You have some reading tasks in a class of ten students.
   e Students are designing an advertisement in groups.
   f The students are going to listen to a tape.
   g You want to explain a grammar point.

D   **What different student groupings can teachers use? [page 20]**

1   Think of three things that students could do in groups of five that they could not do in a whole class of twenty-five.

2   Complete this advantages/disadvantages grid.

	advantages	**disadvantages**
whole class	Teacher can see all the SS	Individual SS don't get enough talking time.
groupwork		
pairwork		
solowork		

3   What's the best grouping for these activities, do you think? Put **W** = Whole class, **P** = Pairwork, **G** = Groupwork, or **S** = Solowork in the boxes.

☐ *Students choose one of three alternatives when faced with an imaginary moral dilemma.*
☐ *Students design a poster for a school event.*
☐ *Students listen to a tape recording of a conversation.*
☐ *Students practise saying sentences with the present perfect ('I've lived here for six years', 'He's studied here for 6 months').*
☐ *Students prepare a talk on a subject of their choosing.*
☐ *Students repeat words and phrases to make sure they can say them correctly.*
☐ *Students work out the answers to a reading comprehension.*
☐ *Students write a dialogue between a traveller and an immigration official.*
☐ *Students write a paragraph about themselves.*
☐ *The teacher explains the rule for the pronunciation of 's' plurals ('pin<u>s</u>, cup<u>s</u>, brush<u>es</u>').*

E   **How can teachers evaluate the success or failure of their lessons? [page 22]**

1   Design a feedback chart for your students to fill in to evaluate one of the following.

a a lesson based on a reading text
b a lesson focusing on grammar work
c a lesson in which students are asked to simulate a job interview

2   Write a list of questions which you would want a colleague to answer about your lesson if you invited him or her in to evaluate an activity or technique.

Chapter 4
How to describe learning and teaching

A   **What do we know about language learning? [page 24]**

1   Complete this chart with as many differences as you can think of
between babies/young children learning their first language and
schoolchildren/adults learning a foreign language in class.

first language	foreign language

2   How like or unlike natural language acquisition was your experience of
learning a foreign language at school?

B   **What elements are necessary for successful language learning in
classrooms? [page 25]**

1   **Engage:** give each of the activities a 'like it' score from 0 (= I don't like
it at all) to 5 (= I love it).

❑ *Students do a puzzle such as matching words to pictures, reassembling
the lines of a poem in the correct order or listening to a tape and trying to
guess what the speaker looks like.*

❑ *Students read a text and give their opinions on it.*

❑ *Students look at an interesting picture as a prelude to some language
work.*

❑ *The teacher comes to class and behaves completely differently from
normal thus creating surprise and interest.*

❑ *The teacher gets students standing in a close circle (or circles). One
student stands in the middle and falls. The others keep him or her upright
– he or she is stopped from falling.*

❑ *The teacher leads a discussion on a controversial topic before giving
students something to read or listen to about it.*

2 **Study:** tick the boxes which are similar to *Study* activities you have experienced as a learner.

☐ *Students listen to the teacher saying individual words and try to hear which syllable is stressed (do we say <u>phot</u>ograph or pho<u>tog</u>raph?). Then they say the words with the correct stress.*

☐ *Students listen to the tone of voice used when saying certain kinds of questions. They practise saying the questions.*

☐ *Students look at a list of words and say which have positive or negative connotations. They make sentences using the words.*

☐ *Students look at examples of comparative adjectives ('better', 'richer', 'bigger', 'friendlier', 'cleverer', 'more interesting', 'more expensive') and on their own try to work out what the rules are for their formation.*

☐ *Students look at six different ways of inviting someone to the cinema. Then they practise saying them.*

☐ *Students look at the present simple tense in detail ('I live', 'you live', 'she lives' etc.) and then practise making sentences with the third person singular ('he, she, it lives/eats/speaks').*

☐ *Students look at the verbs 'make' and 'do'. How are they used? Is there a rule about when you use one or the other? What things do we make? What things do we do?*

3 **Activate:** tick the boxes for the activities you would enjoy doing if you were learning a language.

☐ *Students act out a situation in which one of them goes to a travel agent to buy a ticket.*

☐ *Students design and record a radio advertisement for mobile phones.*

☐ *Students formally debate the issue of whether animals can be said to have rights.*

☐ *Students listen to phone conversations, take messages and then pass them on.*

☐ *Students role-play job interviews: they decide who should get the job.*

☐ *Students work in pairs. One of them has a picture. Without showing it to their partner, they try and get their partner to draw the same picture.*

☐ *Students write a letter to an imaginary agony aunt. Other students write the 'aunt's' reply.*

C **How do the three elements of *ESA* fit together in lesson sequences? [page 27]**

1 How would you describe the following lesson sequences in terms of *ESA*?

A

1 The teacher gives students a number of words and tells them they all come from a story. In groups, the students have to try and work out what the story is.

2 The teacher reads the (ghost) story aloud and the students see if they were right. They discuss whether they like the story.

3 The students now read the story and answer detailed comprehension questions about it.

4 The students look at the use of the past continuous tense (e.g. 'They were sitting at the kitchen table') in the story and make their own sentences using the past continuous.

5 The students talk about ghost stories in general: do they like them/are they scared by them? etc.

6 The students write their own ghost stories.

B

1 The teacher stands in front of the class and starts to look very unhappy. The students are clearly interested/concerned.

2 The teacher mimes feeling ill. The students look like they understand what's going on.

3 The teacher says, 'I'm feeling ill'. The students repeat, 'I'm feeling ill'.

4 The teacher mimes feeling sad/angry/depressed etc., and says, 'I'm feeling sad' etc., and the students repeat the sentences.

5 The teacher models the question 'What's the matter?' The students repeat the question.

6 The students practise questions and answers, e.g. 'What's the matter?' 'I'm feeling depressed' etc.

7 The students do a role-play in which two neighbours meet – and one has just had their car stolen.

C

1 The teacher asks students if they like photographs.

2 The teacher shows students four photographs and puts them in groups to decide which should win a 'photographic competition'.

3 The students question each other about photography – do they own a camera? Do they take a lot of photographs? etc.

4 The students look at a number of words (which will appear in stage 5) and have to decide which part of speech they are.

5 The students look at a poem about a photograph with some of the words blanked out. They have to decide what parts of speech are missing.

6 The students now put their words from stage 4 in the blanks. They listen to a reading of the poem to check that they've got it right.

7 The teacher and the students discuss the meaning of the poem. What's the story? Did they like it?

8 The students write their own poems on a similar theme.

D   **What teaching models have influenced current teaching practice? [page 30]**

Answer these questions after reading the chapter.

a What do the following initials stand for?
   1 CLT   2 PPP   3 TBL
b What connection do the models in (a) have with the following?
   1 Straight Arrows lessons
   2 Boomerang lessons
   3 Patchwork lessons

Chapter 5
How to describe language

A   Sentence constructions [page 35]

1   Identify the elements in the following sentences in terms of **S** (Subject), **V** (Verb), **O** (Object), **C** (Complement) and **A** (Adverbial).

   a He left quickly.
   b She is incredibly intelligent.
   c She read the book very slowly.

   d The school principal wrote a letter.
   e They kissed each other.
   f They will arrive in two hours.

2   Look at the underlined parts of the sentences. Are the verbs transitive or intransitive? What different kinds of object are there?

   a Don't <u>break</u> the cup.
   b He <u>fell</u>.
   c He <u>gave</u> <u>me the letter.</u>
   d It <u>broke</u>.

   e Please <u>sing</u> <u>me that song</u> again.
   f That aftershave <u>smells</u> terrible!
   g They <u>sent</u> <u>the message to their</u> <u>family</u> by e-mail.

B   Parts of speech [page 36]

1   Read the extract on page 149 and then complete the chart below with at least two words from the text for each part of speech.

noun	
pronoun	
adjective	
verb	
adverb	
preposition	
article	
conjunction	

Jeremy Harmer: *How to Teach English* © Addison Wesley Longman 1998
PHOTOCOPIABLE

Matilda said goodnight and set out to walk home to her parents' house, which was about an eight-minute journey away. When she arrived at her own gate, she saw a large black Mercedes motor-car parked outside. She didn't take too much notice of that. There were often strange cars parked outside her father's place. But when she entered the house, she was confronted by a scene of utter chaos. Her mother and father were both in the hall frantically stuffing clothing and various objects into suitcases.

"What on earth's going on?" She cried. "What's happening, daddy?"

"We're off," Mr Wormwood said, not looking up. "We're leaving for the airport in half an hour so you'd better get packed. Your brother's upstairs all ready to go. Get a move on, girl! Get going!"

"Off?" Matilda cried out. "Where to?"

"Spain," the father said. "It's a better climate than this lousy country."

"Spain!" Matilda cried. "I don't want to go to Spain! I love it here and I love my school!"

"Just do as you're told and stop arguing," the father snapped. "I've got enough troubles without messing about with you!"

"But daddy....." Matilda began.

"Shut up," the father shouted. "We're leaving in thirty minutes! I'm not missing that plane."

"But how long for, daddy?" Matilda cried. "When are we coming back?"

"We aren't," the father said. "Now beat it! I'm busy!"

From *Matilda* by Roald Dahl

2   Look at the chart in exercise 1. Add two more words to each category which are not from the text.

C   Noun types [page 36]

1   In the 'Matilda' extract (B1 above), find

    a some countable nouns
    b some uncountable nouns

2   Which different kinds of noun (countable, uncountable, plural nouns, collective nouns) can you put in the blanks?

    a I'd like some _____ .
    b There are two _____ in the story.
    c The _____ is unbelievable.
    d Our _____ are completely crazy!
    e _____ is not only unavoidable, but a good idea too!

Choose words to go in the blanks.

D   Verb types [page 38]

1   Look at the 'Matilda' extract (B1 above) and answer the following questions.

    a How many contracted verb forms can you find? What would the full form be?

b Can you find at least one example of
  1 an auxiliary verb? **2** a main verb? **3** a phrasal verb?

2   What are the underlined verbs – auxiliary, main or phrasal?

  a I *don't* *want* to go to Spain.
  b We*'re* *leaving* in thirty minutes.
  c She *can't* *understand* all the fuss.
  d Matilda *was* *brought up* very badly by her parents.
  e I *might* not *mind*.

E   Verb forms [page 40]

1   Look at the 'Matilda' extract (B1 above) and find one example of each
     of the following.

  a past simple   **c** present simple
  b present continuous   **d** a passive verb

2   Describe the verb forms in these sentences.

  a I haven't seen him for a week.
  b He was being chased by a tiger.
  c I'm enjoying myself.
  d People are usually frightened by the unknown.
  e They were sitting in the early evening sunshine.
  f He had been practising for the game.
  g I get up at about six o'clock every morning – it's terrible!
  h Water! Water! I've been jogging.
  i He finished his drink and walked out of the bar.

F   Pronouns, Adjectives, Adverbs, Prepositions, Articles, Conjunctions and Conditionals [pages 42-6]

1   Explain what is wrong with these student sentences.

  a He bought a French designer red big plastic chair.
  b He himself washed.
  c I like often to play tennis.
  d I love the nature.
  e I'm crazy of French films.
  f The lady sat down beside me was beautiful.
  g She is more bright than her brother.
  h The inhumanity is a terrible thing in our world.
  i In spite of it was late but he started to revise for his exam.
  j I'll see you at Saturday at five o'clock.
  k I have seen him yesterday.

2   Expand this sentence from the 'Matilda extract' (B1 above) using as
     many adverbs and adjectives as you can without the sentence becoming
     impossible. You can use commas, colons, semicolons and hyphens.

  We're leaving for the airport in half an hour so you'd better get packed.

3 Give the 'if' conditions in the following sentences a label saying (a) whether they are 'real' or 'hypothetical' and (b) whether they refer to the present, future or past (e.g. 'real future', 'hypothetical past' etc.).

a If I finish the letter, I'll post it this evening.
b I'd have helped you if you had asked me.
c If you were at all interested, I would tell you about it.
d If you get caught cheating, you have to leave. That's the rule.
e I'll drop in on my way back if I have time.
f If she hadn't fallen asleep, she wouldn't have missed her station.
g If I was clever, I'd know the answer.
h If I got a pay rise, I'd move to a nicer apartment.

G Forms and meanings [page 46]
Language functions [page 48]

1 What different meanings can you think of for the following words, phrases and sentences?

a edge	*f twist*
b end	*g They're off.*
c flag	*h I don't want to miss her.*
d pick	*i It's a goal.*
e shadow	*j They're watching a video.*

2 How many different ways can you think of for expressing the following language functions?

a giving advice	*c offering help*
b inviting someone	*d giving your opinion*

H Words together: collocation [page 48]

1 Which of these words go together? Tick the boxes.

	asleep	awake	alert	conscious
wide				
fast				
fully				
sound				
half				
semi(-)				

2 Use a dictionary or any other source to say what adjectives and/or verbs collocate most frequently with the nouns listed on the next page.

a *cease-fire*	**e** *exam*	**i** *thoughts*
b *crime*	**f** *mouth*	**j** *treaty*
c *criminal*	**g** *muscle*	
d *driver*	**h** *temper*	

I Speaking and writing [page 49]

1   Use the following sentence frame to make as many sentences as possible about the differences between speaking and writing.

Speaking is different from writing because ... .

2   Record an informal conversation between (yourself and) friends in English. Transcribe some of what you hear on the tape and then complete these tasks.

a Take any two lines of transcription and write them out in formal written English.

b Study the transcription. What words are missed out in conversational English?

J Pronunciation [page 50]

1   How many sounds are there in these words?

a activate	*e learner*	*i teacher*
b arrangement	*f overhead projector*	*j willingness*
c classroom	*g performance*	
d emotion	*h rapport*	

2   Write the following words and mark the stress using underlining, stress marks, squares or circles.

a activate	*e export (noun)*	*i Shostakovich*
b adolescent	*f export (verb)*	*j willingness*
c classroom	*g learner*	
d emotion	*h procrastination*	

3   How many different ways can you say the following sentences by changing the stress on the words? What different situations could the sentences be said in?

a It was only last night that you arrived.

b This is not the best art show I've ever attended.

c She's decided she loves you.

4   How many different meanings can you give the following words by changing the intonation?

a well	*c happy*
b no	*d OK*

Chapter 6
How to teach language

A **What does language study consist of? [page 52]**
How should we expose students to language? [page 52]

1   What would be the best way (teacher model, tape, reading passage, something else) of exposing intermediate students to the following language items?

   a the present simple ('I get up at six o'clock', 'She works for the government', 'We play football on Sundays' etc.)
   b ways of agreeing and disagreeing ('Absolutely!' 'Rubbish!' 'I can't agree with you there', 'Oh I do so agree' etc.)
   c words for walking and movement ('stroll', 'limp', 'gallop', 'lurch' etc.)

2   What aspects of grammar and/or vocabulary would the teacher be exposing the students to by showing them the following text?

   It was a dark moonless night. The wind was whistling through the trees and it was raining. The raindrops were hitting his face like knives.
   Suddenly he heard a noise like a scream. It came from his left.
   There was a flash of lightning and a crash of thunder. Then he heard it again. A scream. He ran to the wall and looked over into the graveyard. Someone was digging. In the sudden light of another flash of lightning he saw that it was Jane. Once again the thunder crashed. The parrot on her shoulder screeched.
   That was the noise he had heard. He turned to leave. Someone was standing right behind him. 'Marigold,' he whispered, 'what are you doing here?'

B **How can we help students to understand meaning? [page 55]**

1   How can you make these students understand the meaning of these words?

a to count	*d full*	*g to promise*	*j very*
b confused	*e stagger*	*h under*	
c flower	*f teacher*	*i vehicle*	

2   How can you make students understand the meaning of these language items?

   a ordinal numbers (1st, 2nd, 3rd etc.)
   b 'Do you like X?' 'Yes, I do / No, I don't.'
   c 'going to' future ('I'm going to see my grandmother next week')
   d the first conditional ('If it rains, we'll stay at home', 'If I finish work early, I'll call you')
   e the past continuous ('She was waiting at the station', 'The government was preparing for war' etc.)

Jeremy Harmer: *How to Teach English* © Addison Wesley Longman 1998   **153**
PHOTOCOPIABLE

C   How can we help students to understand language form? [page 56]

1   How would you explain the construction of the following structural items? (You can isolate, distort, use gesture, board diagrams etc.)

   a past tense negatives ('They didn't feel good', 'She didn't go to work' etc.)
   b present simple, 3rd person ('He sleeps', 'she takes', 'It hurts' etc.)
   c superlatives ('best', 'youngest', 'prettiest', 'most alarming' etc.)
   d past passives ('He was seen', 'They were contacted', 'It was designed by ...' etc.)
   e compound words with participles ('walking-stick', 'running shoes', 'sleeping bag' etc.)

2   What can you discover about the word 'effects' by looking at the following concordance?

not randomised failed to show adverse	effects on the baby. Indeed
Dunkirk and Dieppe to offset the adverse	effects of the Tunnel. However
it does matter.) The catastrophic	effects of the most recent drought can be
physical elements. The chemical	effects of burial on the pottery are few
temporary order, to defy the destabilising	effects of time, if only for a moment,
they were protesting at the devastating	effects of the Spanish and Italian drift
evidence was shown of the devastating	effects of bottle feeding where there is
really fragile areas has had disastrous	effects (and some of these are analysed
it has both beneficial and harmful	effects on plants, animals and people.
first to measure the potentially harmful	effects of cosmetics. Although they
regulations of the GATT. These harmful	effects can also be exacerbated by the
saw that even the adults showed no ill	effects at all when I moved the odd
and that it will bring about long-term	effects only if it is repeatedly reinforced
increased research into the long-term	effects of industrial chemicals
this very brutal war is the long-term	effects on children who have been terror
it does possess. The negative	effects of lack of stimulation on visual
is to be performed and its possible	effects to ensure that this does not
her calamity has quite the shattering	effects on personality and behaviour as
two weeks in this patient because of side	effects from the therapy. This is
don't have to worry that it is the side	effects of drugs, as regrettably, some
Rowntree's chapter (1.4) various side	effects of the competitive aspects of
Lawrence does not neglect sound	effects in impressing on us the harsh
judge the general importance of such	effects in controlling long-term behaviour
evidence is coming to light about the	effects of domestic violence on children
sipped her gin, noticing already the	effects the alcohol was having on her.
Sioli (1985) has examined the	effects of deforestation on the soil
from farmers about compensation for the	effects of low flying on livestock
could hardly have transmitted the	effects of international competition to

Edited from the *British National Corpus*

D   **How should students practise language? [page 60]**

Write six model sentences which you could use to practise the following
structures.

a adverbs of manner ('wearily', 'happily', 'longingly' etc.)
b 'must' and 'mustn't' ('You must be quiet, 'You mustn't bring the dog' etc.)
c past simple ('They laughed', 'She cried', 'It happened' etc.)
d prepositions of place ('on', 'in', 'under')
e the present perfect with 'never' ('He's never seen Mount Fuji' etc.)

E   **Why do students make mistakes? [page 62]**
     How should teachers correct students? [page 62]

Complete the blanks with an appropriate form of the correction in the
following exchanges between a teacher and her elementary students.

a TEACHER: *OK ... question, Juan.*
     JUAN: *Where the book is*
     TEACHER: ....

b TEACHER: *Olga?*
     OLGA: *He never has been see Paris.*
     TEACHER: *Can anyone help her?*
     STUDENTS: *He never has see / He never been / He never sees etc.*
     TEACHER: ....

c PAULA: *He can to play tennis.*
     TEACHER: . ...

F   **Where do language study activities fit in teaching sequences?**
     [page 64]

1   Design a complete teaching sequence for one of the following items.

   a asking names and introducing each other
   *b the present continuous ('He's listening', 'They're living', 'It's taking place'
      etc.)*
   c crime vocabulary ('commit a crime', 'juvenile crime', 'theft', 'assault' etc.)
   *d past perfect ('They had arrived', 'It had happened', 'We had finished lunch'
      etc.)*
   e liking language ('like, enjoy, love, dislike, hate' etc.)

2   Look at any textbook you can find and answer the following questions.

   a What percentage of the activities in the book are study activities?
   *b How many different ways does the textbook have of getting students to
      study?*
   c Which study activities (in the book) do you like? Which don't you like?
   d What is your opinion of the way the book approaches language study?

Chapter 7
How to teach reading

A   **Why teach reading? [page 68]**

  1   What is your response to the following questions?

   a What reasons are there for getting students to read texts in English?
   b What different elements of English can students study in a reading text?

  2   Complete the following sentences.

   a When I learnt a foreign language, reading was … .
   b I think reading in the foreign language classroom is … .
   c Students need to learn how to read … .

B   **What kind of reading should students do? [page 68]**

  1   Complete this chart with as many examples as you can think of.

authentic materials appropriate for beginner/elementary students	authentic materials not appropriate for beginner/elementary students

  2   Re-write this sentence so that it accurately reflects your own point of view.

   When reading in class, students should only be given texts which are authentic.

C   **What reading skills should students acquire? [page 69]**

   Make a list of reading texts which would be appropriate for students who are performing one of the following skills.

   scanning (searching a text quickly for specific information)
   skimming (reading a text quickly to get the 'general idea')
   reading for detailed information
   reading for pleasure

D **What are the principles behind the teaching of reading? [page 70]**

1 What would you expect to get out of a good reading text

   a *as a teacher?* **b** *as a student?*

2 What have the following concepts got to do with using reading texts?

   active skill appropriate tasks engagement exploitation prediction response to content

E **What do reading sequences look like? [page 71]**

1 Look at the reading text(s) and complete the tasks which follow it.

YOUR SLEEP AND YOU

MIRIAM KELLAWAY REPORTS

How much beauty sleep do you need? According to Philip Sedgewick, research fellow at the Sleep Disorders Clinic at the Department of Mental Health at St George's Hospital, most of us need roughly eight hours a night if we want to stay healthy. And we need to have a regular routine too.

Problems for tired people:
- more chance of bugs and infections
- shift workers (people who work at different times of day and night) get more infectious diseases than the rest of us
- more chance of stress
- more need for energy food like chocolate, coffee etc. Students in the USA say tiredness causes overeating. In a survey of hospital nurses across the country, ninety percent of those working on the night shift gained weight
- irritability, grumpiness

Canadian sleep researcher Harvey Modofsky, at the Toronto Western Hospital took blood from sleeping people and he found that sleeping bodies were fighting infection better than those that were awake and in a recent study of 9,000 adults in the UK those who slept between six and a half and eight and a half hours a night were more healthy than those who slept less.

REM & Non-REM
- REM stands for Rapid Eye Movement. That's the time we dream, when we sort out all the memories, thoughts and feelings in our head. Non-REM is often called Deep Sleep.
- Without REM people become forgetful, irritable and less able to concentrate.
- Deep sleep provides us with physical and mental recovery.

Things not to do in bed (according to sleep experts):
- eat
- read
- watch television
- work
- drink caffeine
- smoke cigarettes
- have alcohol (it interferes with REM sleep. It can make you tired and irritable the morning after the night before).

Jeremy Harmer: *How to Teach English* © Addison Wesley Longman 1998   **157**
PHOTOCOPIABLE

    a What level do you think it might be suitable for?

    b What kind of comprehension tasks could you do with it?

    c How would you get students Engaged with the topic of the text?

    d What language, if any, would you focus the students' attention on in the reading text for a Study exercise?

    e What would you do after the students had read the text?

2   Can you think of answers to these reading-related questions?

    a What kind of Engage activity would you use before students read a text about rock music?

    b What follow-up activity might you use after your intermediate students have read a text about animal rights?

    c Where would you look for 'authentic' reading material for your beginner students? What would they be able to cope with?

    d Write a mock car advertisement as a reading text for beginner students. How easy is it? What problems did you have doing it?

Chapter 8
How to teach writing

A   **Why teach writing? [page 79]**
       What kind of writing should students do? [page 80]

1   What is the best writing task you can think of for intermediate students
   of English?

2   Put these writing activities in an order of preference for you and a group
   of intermediate students.

   ☐ *filling in a university application form*
   ☐ *imaginary 'agony column' letters*
   ☐ *magazine advertisement*
   ☐ *narrative – autobiographical*
   ☐ *poems*
   ☐ *postcards*
   ☐ *poster for an imaginary amateur drama production*
   ☐ *report on eating – people's habits*
   ☐ *script for an imaginary soap-opera episode*
   ☐ *students re-writing statements to reflect their own views*

B   **What do writing sequences look like? [page 80]**

   Look at these two writing activities for students and give your views on
   these questions.

   a *Would you feel confident using them as a teacher? Why? Why not?*
   b *What problems, if any, can you anticipate for these activities?*
   c *What would you do before the activities to ensure that they were a success?*

   1 upper intermediate

   > **3**   You are going to write an entry for the *Local customs* section of
   > a tourist brochure, talking about the customs and manners of people
   > in your country and giving advice to visitors (e.g. *If possible visitors
   > should ...; Take care to ...; Make sure you ...; Visitors should be careful not
   > to ...; It is unwise to ...; It is never a good idea to...*). Include at least two
   > examples of bad advice but pretend it is good advice (e.g. *Never tip
   > taxi drivers; Feel free to smoke downstairs on buses.*) Divide your notes
   > into paragraphs and write a draft.

   From *Upper Intermediate Matters* by Jan Bell and Roger Gower

2   beginners

> **Read the rules before you play this game.**
> Rules
> 1 Work in pairs. Write four sentences describing another person in the class.
> 2 Don't write the person's name. Write *she* or *he*.
> 3 Write about their appearance, colour of eyes and hair, clothes, job, etc.
> 4 Say where she/he is sitting in the class.
> 5 Number the sentences 1–4. Begin with the most difficult sentence for other people to guess.
> 6 Now read your description, sentence by sentence. How soon can the class guess who you are describing?

From *the Beginners' Choice* by Sue Mohamed and Richard Acklam

C   How should teachers correct writing? [page 84]

1   Re-write the following paragraph so that it reflects your own opinions.

Teachers should correct all the mistakes they find in a student's written work. They should underline the mistakes in red ink. Students should be made to write out the work again.

2   Correct the following piece of writing by an elementary student bearing in mind (a) the need to be encouraging as well as helpful and (b) the usefulness of your correction for the student.

> I am learning English because it's the first
> foring for language for most pepole in
> the world.
> Every body have to use English, in Bank,
> hospital, University, any were yo go you
> have to use it.
> For me, I think English is important
> to reading, speaking, also for writing.
> Most pepole in the world speake English
> were ever they go. Also communcation
> between pepole and cuontery
> cuontery hapend by using English language.

D　What can be done about handwriting? [page 84]

1　Which of the following examples of student handwriting need(s) specialist help in your opinion?

> AT MOMENT I AM SINGLE BUT I HAVE HAD TWO IMPORTAN STORIES FOR FOUR AND FIVE YEARS, NOW I HOPE TO BE FREE LONGER BECCAUSE I AM ENJOYING TOO MUCH. SPORT IS MY LIFE, I LIKE EVERY SPORTS TO WATCA AND PRACTISE.

> Now, Iam going to write about what I do in my travel.
> I stayed for 2 weeks, I went a beach all days, all day wore very nice and very hot.
> I went to shop and I saw many clothes that I liked, I wanted to buy all but I couldn't, I bougth a jacket because I trated to buy clothes that I'll use in London.

> In my spare time, I love travelling and Reading last year I went to Egypt France and Houlland. I also like to Listening to music, walking. I like to play Foot ball.

2　What would you say to the student(s) whose handwriting caused you concern?

E　How does writing fit into *ESA*? [page 85]

Look at the following description of a writing task for intermediate students and answer the questions which follow.

Students are going to write a discursive essay on one of the following topics: 'Is the pen mightier than the sword?', 'Patriotism is the last refuge of the scoundrel'.

They should use a basic four-paragraph structure, e.g. introduction – points in favour – points against – conclusion (including personal opinion).

They should use some or all of the following language: 'Some people think that ...', 'Critics of ... say that ...', 'In my opinion, ...' etc.

How would you get students to do the task if you wanted to

a　*teach a straight arrows lesson (Engage-Study-Activate)?*
b　*organise a boomerang lesson (Engage-Activate-Study ...)?*
c　*include it in a patchwork lesson (where the elements occur in a variety of different orders)?*

Chapter 9
How to teach speaking

A   **What kind of speaking should students do? [page 87]**
Why encourage students to do speaking tasks? [page 87]

1   What should the characteristics of a speaking activity be? Put a tick (√)
    or a cross (x) in the boxes if you agree or disagree with them.

☐ *It should be a Study exercise.*
☐ *It should be an Activate exercise.*
☐ *It should Engage students.*
☐ *It should involve everyone.*
☐ *It should practise specific language structures.*
☐ *Students should concentrate on the accuracy of what they are saying.*

2   Which is the odd one out? Why?

a *a role-play   a discussion   a drill   a communication game*
    a questionnaire
b *a letter   a speech   a poem   a grammar exercise   a play extract*
c *study   rehearsal   feedback   engagement   enjoyment*

B   **What do speaking activities look like? [page 88]**

Look at these two speaking activities for students and give your views
on these questions.

a *Would you feel confident using them as a teacher? Why? Why not?*
b *What problems, if any, can you anticipate for these activities?*
c *What would you do before the activities to ensure that they were a success?*

1   intermediate

> Roleplay
> Work in pairs. Student A – you are a happy vegetarian.
> Student B – you are a happy meat-eater. You have five
> minutes to try to convince each other that your way of
> thinking is the right one.

From *Accelerate Intermediate* by Patricia Lodge and Beth Wright-Watson

2   Elementary

2 Work in pairs.

Student A: You work at the Lost Luggage Office at an airport. Try to identify your partner's suitcase from the suitcases below. Ask about colour, size and material.

Student B: You are at an airport and can't find your suitcase. Turn to page 121.

Student B

Unit 10 Development

EXERCISE 2
You are at the Lost Luggage Office at an airport. You can't find your suitcase. Describe your suitcase (right) to the airport official.

From *Look Ahead Students' Book 2* by Andy Hopkins and Jocelyn Potter

C **How should teachers correct speaking? [page 94]**
What else should teachers do during a speaking activity?
[page 94]

Choose the answer which sounds best to you in each case.

a When teachers hear a mistake during a speaking activity they should
   1 correct it immediately.
   2 ignore it.
   3 note it down and correct it later.
   4 wait for a suitable moment in the activity and then correct it.

b After a speaking activity teachers should
   1 discuss how well the students performed the activity, including comments
      on the content and the language used.
   2 praise the students, not criticise them.
   3 talk about the content of the activity and the achievement of the task,
      but not the language used.
   4 talk about the content of the activity before discussing mistakes.

c When teachers discuss mistakes after a speaking activity they should
   1 give the class examples of language which was used and ask them to say
      if there are any mistakes and if so what they are.
   2 indicate the mistakes to the students who made them.
   3 tell the class that a mistake has been made but not who made it.
   4 write notes to individual students detailing their mistakes.

D **How do speaking activities fit into *ESA*? [page 95]**

Which activities are speaking activities in the following sequences?
What order would you put the activities in? Why?

a
   1 Students discuss whether smoking should be allowed in public places.
   2 Students dictate a poem about smoking to each other.
   3 Students practise making sentences with like/hate verbs
      ('enjoy/love/can't stand' etc.).
   4 Students write letters to a paper about smoking.

b
   1 Students role-play a scene in which a traveller asks for information at a
      railway station.
   2 Students study present simple questions, e.g. 'When does the train leave?',
      'Which is the platform for ...?'
   3 Students listen to station announcements.
   4 Students study railway/timetable-related vocabulary.
   5 Students discuss which form of transport they like best.

Chapter 10
How to teach listening

A   **Why teach listening? [page 97]**

1   How many varieties of English can you think of

  a *in the world?*   *d* *in Africa?*
  b *in Europe?*   *e* *in North America?*
  c *in the Pacific?*

2   Name three reasons for using taped listening material in class and three difficulties which teacher and students might encounter with taped material.

B   **What kind of listening should students do? [page 98]**

1   Complete this chart about types of listening.

	advantages	disadvantages
authentic listening material		
specially written listening materials for language learners		

2   If you were learning a new foreign language, what kind of listening would be most useful for you, do you think?

C   **What's special about listening? [page 98]**

Use the following sentence frame to make as many sentences as possible about the differences between listening and reading.

Listening is different from reading because ... .

D   **What are the principles behind the teaching of listening? [page 99]**

1   What would you expect to get out of a listening exercise as
 a *a teacher?*   *b* *a student?*

2   You are going to use a tape in class for the first time with that tape, that machine and that classroom. How would you prepare before the lesson?

E What do listening sequences look like? [page 101]

Read the following tapescript and complete the tasks which follow it.

ASSISTANT: Can I help you?
OLLIE: Yes, please. I'm looking for some suncream.
ASSISTANT: What kind do you want?
OLLIE: I'm not really sure.
ASSISTANT: Well, the thing to do is decide what factor you need.
OLLIE: What factor?
ASSISTANT: Yes. Choose the right factor and it'll protect you from UV rays.
OLLIE: Ultraviolet rays?
ASSISTANT: Yeah. All you have to do is select the factor which fits your colouring and skin type.
OLLIE: OK. I mean I'm the kind of person who burns quite easily. But I tan in the end.
ASSISTANT: Well, start with this factor 15 and when you've gone brown a bit you can gradually reduce the strength to, I don't know, about 8.
OLLIE: Oh right. So I buy both of these?
ASSISTANT: Yes. That would be a good idea.
OLLIE: How much are they?
ASSISTANT: Six pounds fifty.
OLLIE: Each?
ASSISTANT: Yes.
OLLIE: That's really expensive. I wasn't expecting ... .
ASSISTANT: You want to protect yourself against skin cancer or not?
OLLIE: Yes, of course.
ASSISTANT: Well ... .
OLLIE: Oh, OK. Here you are.
ASSISTANT: Thanks. That's seven pounds change.
OLLIE: Thanks.
ASSISTANT: Enjoy your sunbathing.
OLLIE: If I can afford it ... .

a What level do you think this tapescript could be used with?
b How would you Engage students with the topic? What preparation would you do with the students before they listened to this extract?
c What general listening task would be appropriate for this tapescript?
d What Study activity would be appropriate for this activity?
e Can you think of an Activate stage to follow this listening activity?
f Would you use this tape? Why? Why not?

F Where does video fit in? [page 108]

What reasons can you think of for asking students to do one or all of the following?
a watching the picture without the sound
b listening to the sound without the picture
c freezing the picture
Describe the process you might use for one of these.

Chapter 11
How to use textbooks

A **What are the different options for textbook use? [page 111]**
What do adding, adapting and replacing look like? [page 112]

Look at the extract from an intermediate textbook on page 168 and do
the following tasks.

a What is the aim/are the aims of the lesson?
*b What should/might students be able to do at the end of the lesson that they
were not able to do at the beginning?*
c If you were going to replace any part of the lesson, which would it be?
d What adaptations, if any, would you make to the page?
e What additions, if any, would you make to the lesson?

B **So why use textbooks at all? [page 116]**

1 Complete these sentences.

a When I learnt a foreign language at school the textbook ... .
b The best kind of textbooks for a language student ... .
c If I wrote a textbook, I ... .

2 Complete this chart about using textbooks.

advantages of textbook use	disadvantages of textbook use

3 Will/Do you use a textbook a lot, often, sometimes, rarely or not at all?

READING

1 You're going to read a passage by John Hatt, an experienced traveller, about the things he never leaves home without. Can you decide why he might take the following things?

torch   maps   neck pillow   binoculars
insect repellent   door wedge   earplugs
teaspoon   light bulb

2 Read the passage and match the items in 1 with the descriptions.

3 Answer the questions about difficult vocabulary.

trapped – Is this likely to mean that in the dark without a torch you can or can't escape? (paragraph 1)

banned – If books are difficult to find are they likely to be legal or illegal? (paragraph 3)

minimal – Is it likely to take up a lot or very little room? (paragraph 5)

unscrewed – Does this mean something like take out or put in the old bulb? (paragraph 7)

4 Work in pairs. Can you remember why he takes each item? Read the passage again and check.

He takes earplugs in case there is a lot of noise.

SPEAKING

1 Work in pairs. Talk about equipment you usually take on a car journey, a skiing trip, or a walking holiday. Explain why you take each item using the zero conditional, *in case* and *if*.

2 Is there anything you never leave home without? Make a list of the things you have in your handbag, briefcase or wallet. Which items are essential?

1   In certain places it becomes an everyday tool, and in case of emergencies it is essential. After the bomb explosion at the Grand Hotel in Brighton, Mrs Thatcher started a habit of keeping one by her bed. She had discovered that you are trapped in the dark without one.

2   These often can't be bought after your journey has begun. Even where there are bookshops, buy them before you go in case the best ones are out of stock or politically unacceptable and banned.

3   Although they are an entirely unnecessary piece of equipment, I always travel with them. I then know that I stand a chance of getting some sleep. In much of the world, you may be obliged to sleep against the background of a television, juke box and tape recorder all at full volume.

4   It takes up minimal room and is useful in case you want to eat snacks during journeys or in a hotel room. If you're equipped with a penknife as well, you can eat almost anything.

5   They are useful in cheap hotels, in case you can't lock the door from the inside; sleeping friends have been robbed by thieves entering through the bedroom door.

6   On my first evening in Cuba I had dinner with a friend who had just spent three weeks there. She gave me one, claiming that it was one of the best presents I would ever get. She was correct. Every evening I unscrewed the miserable, dim one in my hotel room and replaced it with the 150 watt one. This cheered up the room and, more important, enabled me to read.

7   If you don't get the window seat on a train, bus or plane, falling asleep can be uncomfortable: when nodding off, your head suddenly lolls uncomfortably to one side. In recent years blow-up ones have been widely marketed, and can be found in big stores or airport shops. With one of these you can sleep comfortably on any transport.

From *Reward Intermediate* by Simon Greenall

C How should teachers choose textbooks? [page 117]

Choose any textbook and complete this chart with comments about it.

area	comments
1 price Students' Book? Other components? Appropriate for teacher and students?	
2 availability All components? Next and previous levels?	
3 layout and design Attractive? User-friendly design?	
4 methodology *ESA* opportunities? Study and activation balance?	
5 skills Coverage? Balance? Study <u>and</u> Activation?	
6 syllabus Appropriate? Coverage? Sequence?	
7 topic (culturally) Appropriate? Appropriate level? Varied?	
8 stereotyping People treated equally? Racism, sexism? etc.	
9 teacher's guide Clear? Useful? Answers?	

Compare your comments with a colleague.

Chapter 12
How to plan lessons

A   **Why plan at all? [page 121]**
What are the aims of a plan? [page 122]
What should be in a plan? [page 122]
What questions do we need to ask? [page 123]

1   Make a list of any written or mental plans you make in your daily life
(e.g. shopping lists etc.). What do you use them for? How useful are
they?

2   Rate the following statements 0 (= totally disagree) to 5 (= totally
agree).

a Lesson plans restrict teachers when they are in the classroom.   ❏

*b Teachers should spend more time making good plans than actually
teaching.*   ❏

*c If an activity is worth doing (e.g. an enjoyable language drill),
it's worth spending some time doing it – e.g. for 45 of 50 minutes.*   ❏

*d It doesn't really matter what's in the plan so long as there is lots
of variety in it.*   ❏

*e The most important thing about an activity in the plan is that it
should have the potential to amuse the students.*   ❏

B   **What form should a plan take? [page 125]**

Study the lesson plan on page 171 and answer these questions.

a Do you like the lesson?
b Is it a good plan? What would you leave out? What would you add?
c How useful would the plan be for an observer?

Jeremy Harmer: *How to Teach English* © Addison Wesley Longman 1998

LESSON PLAN	Time [" = minutes]
Description of Class elementary/lower intermediate: 20 students Difficult to make them take part in speaking activities and things like that. They can be very bad tempered especially if they've been out the night before (because it's a morning class).	
Aims to teach comparatives fluency practice writing practice (if time)	3" 5"
Procedure 1 T tells story about a terrible journey – plane.	5"
2 SS in groups. T tells them to discuss transport. Which do they prefer? Which do they dislike? SS report back to class.	
3 T gets SS to look at article title. Asks them what it's going to be about. SS read article. Were they correct?	
4 SS do ex 5 on page 24.*	5"

5 SS do ex 6 & 7.
  Problems?
  sounds: /tʃ/ cheaper
  stress: <u>com</u>fortable, con<u>ven</u>ient/im<u>port</u>ant
	10"

6 T models sentence 'Trains are cheaper than planes'. Choral & individual
  repetition.
  Controlled practice of following sentences:
  Trains are better than planes.
  Trains are cheaper than planes.
  Trains are safer than planes.
  Trains are more comfortable than planes.
  and then reversed, e.g. Planes are more expensive than trains.
  Problems? Sentence stress: 3-hit rhythm (weak 'are' ,'-er' and 'than').
  Example: <u>Trains</u> are <u>cheap</u>er than <u>planes</u>.
	10"

7 T elicits vocabulary to describe furniture.
  T tells SS they are in a furniture store. Have to decide on which sofa to
  buy (see attached role cards).
  SS role-play in pairs.
	15"

8 (if time) Pairs write imaginary fax to their partner with information and advice about sofa purchase.	10"
Comments The students may not be prepared to talk about transport or role-play the furniture store. T will encourage them. Some SS may know comparatives. If so T will miss out controlled practice stage.	

*Page and exercise numbers refer to *Look Ahead Students Book 2* by Andy
Hopkins and Jocelyn Potter (see pages 53, 56, 58-9, 61, 63 and 65 of this
book for the exploitation of the material mentioned here).

Role cards

Role card A
You and your partner want to buy a sofa – preferably a 3-seater. Your partner has sent you to check out what's available.
You are especially interested in comfort – and you like the Handsruff design, if possible. You want to spend around £450 to £600.

Role Card B
You work in the furniture department of a big store. Greet your customer and give them information which they require.

make	2-seaters	3-seaters
Convivum	£310 Comfort **	£514 Comfort ***
Handsruff	£525 Comfort ****	£630 Comfort ****
Harley-Robertson	£620 Comfort *****	£765 Comfort *****
Natch	£499 Comfort ***	£570 Comfort ***

C   How should teachers plan a sequence of lessons? [page 125]

1   Complete the following sentences with as many ideas as possible.

Planning a sequence of lessons is a good idea because ...
Planning a sequence of lessons is a bad idea because ...

Which sentence has the most completions?

2   Make a rough plan (with approximate times) for a sequence of five lessons of fifty minutes each. Details of the class are as follows.
* *The lessons take place from 11.00–11.50 every weekday morning.*
* *There are twenty students in the class. Age range 17-28. 11 women, 9 men. A mixture of students and young professionals.*
* *They are elementary students.*
* *They 'know' the verb 'to be' (past and present), numbers, days, dates and most times. They 'know' a number of question words, they can perform introductions etc.*
* *Among the things you want to cover are: the present simple, maybe with adverbs of frequency, functional dialogues asking for information (e.g. about timetables), descriptions of lifestyles etc.*

Chapter 13
What if?

A   **What if students are all at different levels? [page 127]**

1   Re-write these sentences so that they reflect your own opinion.

   a Mixed ability classes present the teacher with insuperable problems.
   b The only thing you can do with a mixed ability class is ignore the problem.
   c All classes are mixed ability classes.

2   How would you approach these tasks with a mixed ability group?

   a You want to use the Eddie Edwards tape on page 107 with your students.
   b You want students to write a ghost story, having studied storytelling, and having been given some 'ghost' vocabulary and phrases.
   c You want students to study ways of agreeing and disagreeing – and later use them, if possible, in some kind of discussion.
   d You have a poem which you want students to look at. You can refer to 'Fire and Ice' on page 76-7 if you want.
   e Three of your good students are making it clear that they're finding your classes too easy for them.
   f You want to hand back some written work and deal with the mistakes that you found when correcting.

B   **What if the class is very big? [page 128]**

1   Complete this chart. In the first column, write things you can do with small classes (ten or under) but you can't do with big classes (of forty plus). In the second column, write things you can do with big classes which you can't do with small classes.

small classes	big classes

2   In big classes, what special considerations need to be taken into account for the following?
   a the teacher's voice
   b the teacher's place in the class
   c the teacher's board work / overhead projector use
   d using the tape recorder

C   What if students keep using their own language? [page 129]

1   What action can teachers take if students use their own language in class all the time? List as many things as you can think of.

2   In which of the following situations, if any, would you let students use their own language?

   a   Students are working in pairs to practise a dialogue.
   b   Students are debating the issue of whether birth control should be imposed on the world to prevent overpopulation.
   c   Students are working in pairs to solve a reading puzzle.
   d   Students are checking that they understand the instructions for an activity.
   e   Students are doing a group writing task.
   f   Students are taking part in a business meeting simulation.

D   What if students are uncooperative? [page 130]

1   How many ways are there for students to be uncooperative in class? List them in order where the first one is most difficult for the teacher to deal with and the last is the least challenging for the teacher.

2   What might teachers and students write in this contract form?

THE LANGUAGE-LEARNING CONTRACT	
TEACHER	**LEARNER**
As your teacher I will	As a learner I will
As your teacher I expect	As a learner I expect

E   What if students don't want to talk? [page 131]

1   What reasons can you anticipate for students who don't want to talk and who therefore sit silently in the class? Which are the easiest to deal with? Which are the most difficult?

Jeremy Harmer: *How to Teach English* © Addison Wesley Longman 1998
                                              PHOTOCOPIABLE

2   Copy and complete the chart with ideas for making reluctant speakers talk – and the possible consequences of such actions.

action	consequences
encourage them by picking them out in whole class work	might work, but might make them shyer

F   **What if students don't understand the listening tape? [page132]**

1   What problems do students have (in general) when listening to tapes in class? How can you help them to overcome these difficulties?

2   Look at this transcript of an interview with a pub landlord (for upper intermediate students) and answer these questions.

   a What problems, if any, would you expect students to have with this tape? (The speaker uses a 'southern English standard' variety of English; he speaks reasonably clearly and slowly.)
   b What action would you take to counter these problems?

PADDY: The man you have to watch is the one who becomes quietly belligerent, and you sort of take him gently by the elbow to lead him to the door and the next thing you know is thump – you've been you've been landed one, and of course without warning you have to collect your senses pretty quickly before he lands you another one! Er, there was one gentleman who sat over there; he was wearing a suit, waistcoat, pressed shirt and tie, his hair immaculately groomed – er he did speak with an Irish accent but then there's nothing wrong with that – and I spotted on the second pint of Guinness that he didn't know how to get his money out of his pocket, he was far too gone for that. But he'd got his pint of Guinness and he managed to pay for it, and I thought, when he's finished that one I will say no. But unfortunately he sat with it in front of him and didn't drink it, and ten past eleven came, quarter past eleven came, twenty past eleven came and I said, 'Drink up or lose it because it's time to go home. You know the law as well as I do.' And he said, 'If you touch my blankety blank drink I'll blankety blank work your blankety blank pub over.' So I took his glass away from him and walked to the bar and put it over the side and er left the door open for him to go out, and he swore profusely and started towards the door and I thought that was the end of the matter, I thought he'd gone; went behind the bar to wash up the glass and one or two others that were there, when there was an almighty crash and he'd picked up a chair and hurled it right through the overhead lights which slowed it down, praise be, and it landed on the counter, smashing the glasses that I was waiting to wash. By the time I'd sort of realised what had happened and turned round – that was all in what? half a half a, a second, two seconds – by the time I had turned round he was then staggering out the door still calling me all the blankety blank names you could think of but he'd done the damage. He had gone. There was no point in calling the police. There was no point in making any more issue of it; he had gone. But he still caused quite a lot of damage and er it was quite ... when I realised what might have happened if he hadn't hit the light with the with the chair – yes, quite, I would have got the chair in the back of the neck, literally, but he just aimed it too high and it got tangled up in these hanging lamps that you can see here, got caught up in the chain, and it just slowed it down and it fell onto the counter rather than on me, and er I thought I'd dealt with the situation quite well, but I've learned not to turn my back now. You don't do that.

From *The Listening File* by Jeremy Harmer and Steve Elsworth

G   What if some students-in-groups finish before everybody else? [page 133]

1   What kind of activity could you have 'up your sleeve' to give to groups of students who finish before some of the other groups in the class? Can you think of examples?

2   Look at the 'Fire and Ice' poem activity on pages 76-7. What would you do in these situations?

a One group finish the activity before the others.
b One group still haven't finished the activity even after the rest have.
c One group don't seem to be concentrating on the activity; they are talking about something else.
d One group keep asking you for help to do the activity.
e One group say 'Oh we know this poem' when you give them the sheets of paper.

Appendix A

Equipment in the classroom

The following items of equipment (in alphabetical order) are frequently used in classrooms and study centres.

The board

Many boards are still chalk-based, but white boards (which use marker pens) are also common.

- Boards can be used for anything: writing, drawing, sticking things on, projecting overhead transparencies etc. (if they are whiteboards).
- The two things to remember about boards is that (a) your writing needs to be legible to all the students in the class, and (b) organised boards are better than chaotic ones! Some teachers divide their boards so that a column is kept for new words etc. Many teachers use different coloured pens or chalk to highlight grammar or pronunciation.

Which of the following boards do you prefer? Why?

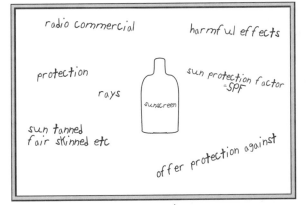

The computer

The range of uses for computers in English language teaching is growing all the time, even as you read this!

- The main thing to make sure of when you get a computer for use in English language teaching is that it has all the functions you require (CD, audio, separate or integral modem etc) and that it is both fast enough and has a big enough memory for the tasks you wish it to perform.

- The main uses for the computer in English language teaching are:

   a as a word processor where students can sit round a screen and put together a text; it is becoming increasingly possible for them to add in graphics and design too
   b as a tool for material specially designed for EFL language games, CDs attached to courses with workbook-type exercises, film clips, interactive listening material etc.
   c as enormous reference tools; not only are there encyclopedias on CDs (Encarta, Grolier) but there are also dictionaries and especially language corpuses which produce material like that for 'protection' on page 54
   d students can use the Internet – either as a way of being in contact with others through e-mail, or for the many other 'talking shops' available on the system or as a source of information on just about every subject under the sun. The facility which allows students to 'talk' to other English speakers from anywhere in the world cannot be praised too highly. See pages 185-6 for some Internet addresses for teachers.

- Of course, the chief problem with computers is their cost, but this is coming down all the time. There is a danger, too, that students will spend too much of their time on the machines and/or that computers will become just as ordinary as everything else. We also have to remember that people working on their own at computer screens can become extremely uncommunicative!

The dictionary

Whether the dictionary is on a computer or in traditional book form, it is the most useful tool the students can use.

- There are a number of excellent EFL dictionaries available at the moment – including ones designed to help students actually produce language rather than just looking up meanings and uses. You need to look for qualities like ease of use, clear presentation, definitions written so that students can understand them, and good typical examples of use.

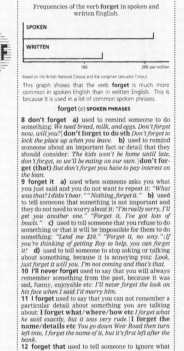

forgetful 552

that letter?" "Oh, sorry, I forgot." | **forget to do sth** *Someone's forgotten to turn off their headlights.* | **forget (that)** *I forgot that I was supposed to come in early this morning.* | **clean forget** (=completely forget) *He meant to invite Monica to the party but he clean forgot.*
3 ► STOP THINKING ABOUT ◄ [I, T] to try to stop thinking and worrying about someone or something that makes you unhappy: *Years after their divorce Olivia still could not forget John.* | **[+ about]** *I'd forget about it if I were you.*
4 ► NOT CARE ABOUT ◄ [I,T] to not care about or give attention to someone or something: **[+ about]** *Don't go off to college and forget about your old friends, okay?*
5 ► STOP A PLAN ◄ [I, T] to stop trying to do something because it is no longer seems possible: **[+ about]** *We'll have to forget about going on holiday.* | *If we can't get any funding we might as well forget the whole thing.*
6 not forgetting used to add something to a list of things: *Bear in mind that we have to pay for all the packaging and transportation costs, not forgetting airport taxes.*
7 forget yourself to do something stupid or embarrassing, especially by losing control of your emotions: *Veronica was worried that she might forget herself and confess her true feelings for him.*

Frequencies of the verb **forget** in spoken and written English.

SPOKEN

WRITTEN

100   200 per million

Based on the British National Corpus and the Longman Lancaster Corpus

This graph shows that the verb **forget** is much more common in spoken English than in written English. This is because it is used in a lot of common spoken phrases.

forget (v) SPOKEN PHRASES

8 don't forget a) used to remind someone to do something: *We need bread, milk, and eggs. Don't forget now, will you?* | **don't forget to do sth** *Don't forget to lock the place up when you leave.* **b)** used to remind someone about an important fact or detail that they should consider: *The kids won't be home until late, don't forget, so we'll be eating on our own.* | **don't forget (that)** *But don't forget you have to pay interest on the loan.*
9 forget it a) used when someone asks you what you just said and you do not want to repeat it: *"What was that? I didn't hear." "Nothing, forget it."* **b)** used to tell someone that something is not important and they do not need to worry about it: *"I'm really sorry, I'll get you another one." "Forget it, I've got lots of bowls."* **c)** used to tell someone that you refuse to do something or that it will be impossible for them to do something: *"Lend me $10." "Forget it, no way."* | *If you're thinking of getting Roy to help, you can forget it!* **d)** used to tell someone to stop asking or talking about something, because it is annoying you: *Look, just forget it will you. I'm not coming and that's that.*
10 I'll never forget used to say that you will always remember something from the past, because it was sad, funny, enjoyable etc: *I'll never forget the look on his face when I said I'd marry him.*
11 I forget used to say that you cannot remember a particular detail about something you are talking about: **I forget what/where/how etc** *I forget what he said exactly, but it was very rude.* | **I forget the name/details etc** *You go down Weir Road then turn left into, I forget the name of it, but it's first left after the bank.*
12 forget that used to tell someone to ignore what you have just said because it is not correct, important

etc: *Then mix the flour with 500 cls of milk, no, forget that, 50 cls of milk.*
13 and don't you forget it used to remind someone angrily about an important fact that should make them behave differently: *Listen, I'm the boss around here, and don't you forget it!*
14 aren't you forgetting...?/haven't you forgotten...? used to tell someone that they have forgotten to consider something important: *"Wait a minute – aren't you forgetting something? No? Well what about saying 'thank you'?"*

for·get·ful /fə'getfəl‖fər-/ adj often forgetting things —**forgetfulness** n [U] —**forgetfully** adv
forget-me-not /·'· ·,·/ n [C] a small plant with pale blue flowers
for·get·ta·ble /fə'getəbəl‖fər-/ adj often humorous not very interesting or good: *a completely forgettable movie*
for·giv·a·ble /fə'gɪvəbəl‖fər-/ adj bad behaviour that is forgivable is not seriously bad and you can easily forgive it: *I suppose a little over-excitement is forgivable under the circumstances.*
for·give /fə'gɪv‖fər-/ v past tense **forgave** /-'geɪv/ past participle **forgiven** /-'gɪvən/ [I,T] **1** to decide not to blame someone or be angry with them although they have done something wrong: *Can you ever forgive me?* | **forgive sb for sth** *I can't forgive him for what he did to my sister.* | **forgive sb sth** *forgive us our sins* | **I'd never forgive myself** *If anything happened to the kids I'd never forgive myself.* | **forgive and forget** (=forgive someone for something and behave as if they had never done it) **2 forgive me** *spoken* used when you are going to say something or ask something that might seem rude or offensive: *Forgive me, Mr Lewis, but I don't think that is relevant.* | *forgive me for saying so, but I think that's nonsense.* **3 sb could be forgiven for thinking/wondering/believing etc sth** used to say that it is easy to understand why someone would think or believe something: *A foreign visitor could be forgiven for thinking football is a religion in this country.* [S]3]
for·give·ness /fə'gɪvn̩s‖fər-/ n [U] the act of forgiving someone: **ask for/beg for forgiveness** (=ask someone to forgive you)
for·giv·ing /fə'gɪvɪŋ‖fər-/ adj willing to forgive: *My father was a kind and forgiving man.*
for·go /fɔː'gəʊ‖fɔːr'goʊ/ v [T] to FOREGO
for·got /fə'gɒt‖fər'gɑːt/ the past tense of FORGET
for·got·ten¹ /fə'gɒtn̩‖fər'gɑːtn/ the past participle of FORGET
forgotten² adj [usually before noun] that people have forgotten about or no longer pay much attention to: *a rare plant growing in a forgotten corner of the churchyard*

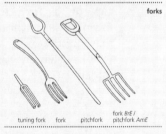

forks

tuning fork   fork   pitchfork   fork BrE / pitchfork AmE

fork¹ /fɔːk‖fɔːrk/ n [C] **1** a tool used for picking up and eating food, with a handle and three or four points: *knives and forks* **2** a garden tool used for digging, with a han-

---

- All classrooms should have a stock of dictionaries. They can be used for students working on a writing task, for example. They can be used when working out meanings of difficult words, when looking for ways of saying things etc. It is important that your students are familiar with ways of using them.
- There are two main worries about dictionaries: the first is that students will buy ones which are inappropriate, ignoring the excellent dictionaries now available especially for them (see page 190) and the second is that they will get to rely on them too much (for example, during reading work, when dictionary use would get in the way of general comprehension). Teachers need to train students in appropriate dictionary use.

The overhead projector

Overhead projectors (OHPs) are really useful for showing pre-prepared overhead transparencies (OHTs) or as an alternative to the board.

- One of the great advantages of an OHP is that you can put a number of OHTs one on top of the other, creating an emerging pattern, e.g.

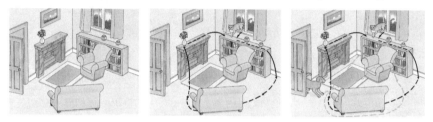

- This ability to put one OHT on top of another allows the teacher to write on top of a text for example without marking the original OHT (which is underneath), e.g.

headlines omit articles etc.

present simple is often used in headlines

NEITHBOUR BITES DOG IN STREET DISPUTE

A 47-year-old man, William Jesperson, bit his neighbour's dog in a dispute about her garden fence yesterday. Mrs Carol Ramsey has complained to the police and her dog needed four stitches.

The argument between William Jesperson and Carol Ramsey started when Mrs Ramsey took down the fence between their two gardens. She told her neighbour she was going to replace it with a newer one but she has not yet done so because she claims she cannot afford to.

When the fence was removed Mrs Ramsey's dog used Mr Jesperson's garden to play in, on one occasion frightening his two-year-old son. Despite repeated complaints Mrs Ramsey had done nothing and when the dog chased Mr Jesperson's pet rabbit, the outraged father and pet-lover took action.

'We are investigating,' says a spokeswoman for Thames Valley Police.

commas used to separate phrase

what do you think?

- Another advantage of the OHP is that by masking the OHT with bits of paper/card etc we can reveal things gradually, e.g.

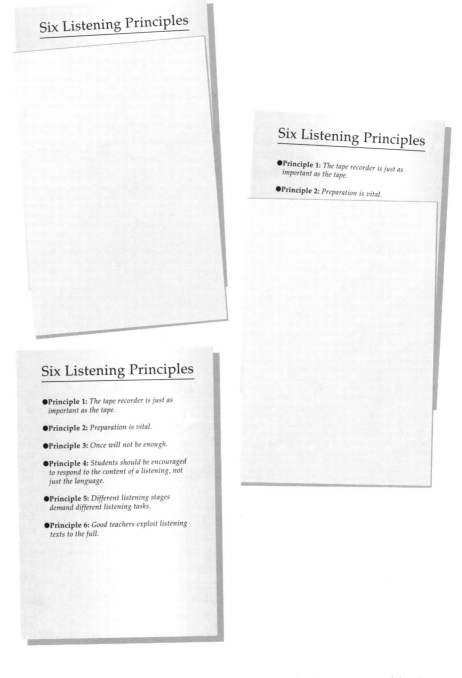

- The two things to watch out for with OHPs is that (a) the writing/designs on the OHTs should be big enough and clear enough for everyone to see and (b) that there should be some surface (a screen, the wall, a board) which is not bleached out by direct sunlight etc.

Pictures and cards

Even in an increasingly technological age, there is still good value to be had from pictures of all shapes and sizes.

- Pictures can come from a variety of sources: drawings, magazines, professionally published material, postcards, photographs etc.
- Teachers can use pictures as prompts for controlled language work – as an alternative to holding up objects like pens – as aids for speaking activities or writing tasks, as a focus for description and discussion (teasing meaning out of a painting, for example) and as visual aids for language structure.
- The things to watch out for with pictures is that they are durable – if they are on cards, for example, the cards should be tough and be properly covered with some kind of laminate so that they can be re-used. They should look good – there's nothing worse than a tatty torn picture from an old magazine – and they should be big enough and visible enough for the students to see.

The tape recorder

In Chapter 10, we looked at tape recorder use for listening material.

- The main thing to remember about tape recorders is that you have to strike a balance between convenience and quality. They may need to be portable, but they also need to be audible. Features to look out for include a good tape counter, easy controls, fast winding and loudness.
- Tape recorders can be used for playing textbook tapes, tapes of people speaking, music tapes (for background, for music-related activities – see page 116 – or for work on songs). They can also be used for students to record themselves (for checking by the teacher, or as part of an activity, e.g. after they have written 'the news' or a radio commercial, for example).
- If it is possible, there are times when it makes sense to have different groups listening to different machines.
- The main disadvantages of tape recorders are that the good ones are often too expensive and rather unwieldy; the bad ones sound terrible. Tapes have a habit of stretching and sticking too. Nevertheless, the better portable machines used with good quality tape are incredibly useful and versatile.

The video playback machine

In Chapter 10, we looked briefly at the use of videos in the classroom.

- The main thing you need to think about for video playback machines and their monitors is that the monitors need to be big enough and in the right place so that everyone can see them. They must have good speakers so that they can be properly heard. The playback machine needs to be of good quality too. The functions to look for include a good remote control device, fast winding and clear 'freeze frame' devices.
- Video can be used for many things: presenting information, giving background to a topic, playing various forms of dialogues and interactions, lectures, and any output from TV channels – the whole range of documentaries, news programmes, dramas, comedies, game shows etc.
- Video loses its impact if it is over-used and teachers tend to find that students lose their (intellectual) focus if they watch too much – just like the soporific television watcher, the famous 'couch potato'.
- The main disadvantage of video machines and their tapes is that frequently the latter don't seem to give the clarity of the original. The other thing you have to be careful about are the copyright laws. You need to check what you can tape from the TV. There may also be rules about showing movies in a fee-paying environment etc.

The video camera

Video cameras are incredibly useful in the EFL classroom.

- The main thing you need to look out for is ease of use (if inexperienced people are going to use them) and good microphones. There's no point in recording students if you can't hear what they say.
- Video cameras have two main uses in the classroom: in the first, the teacher films the students doing an activity. She can then play the tape so that she and the students can discuss the activity. Who said or did successful things? Why didn't a certain piece of English work? What was wrong about the way a student delivered a talk etc.?

- The second use of video cameras is for the students to make films as part of a project or an activity. They can record their own news broadcasts or documentaries. They can record and perform their own play or soap opera. They can take the camera out onto the street to go and interview people. In the planning and execution of these tasks, a lot of good English is learned and used.

- There are a number of things to watch out for with video cameras/camcorders. Firstly, you need to be able to use them properly, so some training for teacher and students is a good idea. The second danger to watch out for is that students don't take the situation seriously enough and just fool around with the camera. Lastly, we have to make sure that a student doesn't get stuck behind the camera – and therefore lose out on chances to practise English.

Notes and further reading

- **Teachers' associations**
- **Journals for teachers**
- **Further reading, chapter by chapter**

Teachers' associations

Two important teachers' associations are The International Association of Teachers of English as a Foreign Language (IATEFL), 3 Kingsdown Chambers, Kingsdown Park, Tankerton, Whitstable, Kent CT5 2DJ, UK [e-mail IATEFL@compuserve.com, web site http://www.iatefl.org] and Teachers of English to Speakers of Other Languages (TESOL), 1600 Cameron Street, Suite 300, Alexandria, Virginia 22314, USA [e-mail tesol@tesol.edu, web site http://www.tesol.edu]. However, most countries have their own organisations which are frequently just as relevant, if not more so, to the needs of teachers working there.

Journals for teachers

Most countries have their own journals. Examples are *TESOL in Context* (Australia), *ELT News and Views* (Argentina), *JALT News* (Japan) or *Israel English Teaching Journal* (Israel). Such journals are always worth looking at since they will often reflect local realities more accurately than international publications.

The UK journals which it is well worth reading on a regular basis are *ELT Journal*, published by Oxford University Press, *Modern English Teacher*, published by Prentice Hall Europe, and *English Teaching Professional* published by First Person Publishing.

The two US journals which teachers will want to look at are *English Teaching Forum* published by the United States Information Service and available through US embassies and *TESOL Journal* (see the address for TESOL above).

At the time of writing there is a large number of sites on the INTERNET where teachers can discuss teaching issues. Web sites are being created all the time but four places to start looking are:

TES-L – available via e-mail at TESL-L@CUNYVM.CUNY.EDU. This is a place where you can take part in discussions about any and many issues related to English language teaching. It has over 12,000 subscribers, we are told.

The Internet TESL Journal at http://www.aitech.ac.jp/~iteslj. This has links to many other sites.

Dave's ESL Cafe at http://www.pacificnet.net/~sperling / elscafe.ntml. This site is just stuffed full of information and articles and links all over the place.

Addison-Wesley Longman at http://awl.elt-com/ – not just this publisher's web site, but also a place for discussion about ELT issues, news and views.

Further reading, chapter by chapter

The following reading suggestions are arranged chapter by chapter. The books mentioned reflect only a fraction of the many published works on the topics in question. But all of the books mentioned here make reference to other books and in such a way a search can be started!

All good publishers have a methodology list and/or applied linguistics list so it worth consulting them. Alternatively, a specialised ELT bookshop will be able to help, as will a visit to your local library.

Frequent mention is made of my book *The Practice of English Language Teaching*. This is because it is the elder sibling of this present volume.

Chapter 1 How to be a good teacher

On what it is to be a **teacher**, read Scrivener, J *Learning Teaching*. Heinemann 1994, Chapter 1 and Brown, S and McIntyre, D *Making Sense of Teaching* Open University Press 1993 – an account of research into the topic.

On **variety and flexibility**, the weighty Fanselow, J *Breaking Rules*. Longman 1987 is a hard read but makes a convincing case for surprising students and teachers!

Chapter 2 How to be a good learner

On **motivation**, see Ur, P *A Course in Language Teaching*. Cambridge University Press 1996, module 19 and Harmer, J *The Practice of English Language Teaching* new edition. Longman 1991, Chapter 1.

On **self access** (students taking responsibility for their own learning), see Sheerin, S *Self Access*. Oxford University Press 1989.

On **learner training**, have a look at all the exercises in Ellis, G and Sinclair B, *Learning to Learn English*. Cambridge University Press 1989. This was the groundbreaking work in this area.

On **teaching adults**, see Rodgers, A *Teaching Adults*. Open University Press 1986.

Chapter 3 How to manage teaching and learning

For more on the various issues of **classroom management** mentioned here, read Gower, R, Phillips, D and Walters, S *Teaching Practice Handbook* new edition. Heinemann 1995, Underwood, M *Effective Classroom Management.* Longman 1987, and Harmer, J *The Practice of English Language Teaching* new edition. Longman 1991, Chapter 11.

Chapter 4 How to describe teaching and learning

On **grammar-translation** and **audio-lingualism**, (and on the history of language teaching in general) it is worth reading Howatt, A *A History of English Language Teaching.* Oxford University Press 1984.

On **PPP**, read Byrne, D **Teaching Oral Skills** new edition. Longman 1986.

On **Task-Based Learning**, the book to read is Willis, J *A Framework for Task-Based Learning.* Longman 1996.

For more on **Communicative Language Teaching**, have a look at Nunan, D *Designing Tasks for the Communicative Classroom.* Cambridge University Press 1989.

A **lexical approach** is argued for in Lewis M *The Lexical Approach.* Language Teaching Publications 1993.

For a different way of **describing teaching elements**, see Jim Scrivener in *Learning Teaching.* Heinemann 1994. Pages 133–138.

For more on the special features of **spoken English**, see Carter, R and McCarthy, M *Exploring Spoken English.* Cambridge University Press 1997.

For more on various **learning and teaching theories**, it's well worth reading the provocative articles in Willis, D and Willis, J (editors) *Challange and Change in Language Teaching.* Heinemann 1996. See also Harmer, J *The Practice of English Language Teaching* new edition. Longman 1991. Chapter 9.

Chapter 5 How to describe language

The two **grammars** I recommend are Swan, M *Practical English Usage* new edition. Oxford University Press 1995, and Alexander, L *Longman English Grammar.* Longman 1988.

On **vocabulary** (and vocabulary teaching), read the exceptional Gairns, R and Redman, S *Working with Words.* Cambridge University Press 1986 and McCarthy, M *Vocabulary.* Oxford University Press 1990. See also Harmer, J *The Practice of English Language Teaching* new edition. Longman 1991, Chapter 9.

On **pronunciation,** have a look at Kenworthy, J *Teaching English Pronunciation.* Longman 1987 or Dalton, C and Seidlhoffer, B *Pronunciation.* Oxford University Press 1994. On aspects of pronunciation teaching methodology, it's also well worth reading Underhill, A *Sound Foundations.* Heinemann 1994

Chapter 6 How to study language

On various kinds of **study activity,** see Byrne, D *Teaching Oral Skills new edition.* Longman 1986 (for a more traditional approach), Harmer, J *The Practice of English Language Teaching* new edition. Longman 1991, Chapter 6 and Scrivener, J *Learning Teaching.* Heinemann 1994, Chapter 9.
On **correcting students** in general, see Edge, J *Mistakes and Correction.* Longman 1989, especially Chapter 5 for correction during accuracy work.

For the use of **concordances** in the classroom (such as the 'protection' example), see Tribble, C and Jones, G *Concordancing in the Classroom.* Longman 1990. Concordance software includes the Longman *Mini Concordancer* published by Addison Wesley Longman and *WordSmith Tools* published by Oxford University Press. You can also get some readable concordances in book form from Collins CoBuild/Heinemann (they are called *Concordance samplers*) and you can get up-to-date information and examples from the CoBuild web site at http://titania.cobuild.collins.co.uk/

On various kinds of **discovery activity,** see Hall, N and Shepheard, J *The Anti-Grammar Grammar Book.* Longman 1991 and Bolitho, R and Tomlinson, B *Discover English* new edition. Heinemann 1994.

Chapter 7 How to teach reading

On **teaching the 'four skills'** in general (which applies to this and the next four chapters), see Gower, R, Phillips, D and Walters, S *Teaching Practice Handbook* new edition. Heinemann 1995, Chapter 5.

On **reading** in general, see Grellet, F *Developing Reading Skills.* Cambridge University Press 1981, Ur, P *A Course in Language Teaching.* Cambridge University Press 1996, Module 10 and Harmer, J *The Practice of English Language Teaching* new edition. Longman 1991, Chapter 10.

Chapter 8 How to teach writing

On **writing** in general, read Byrne, D *Teaching Writing Skills* new edition. Longman 1988, Tribble, C *Writing.* Oxford University Press 1996, and Harmer, J *The Practice of English Language Teaching* new edition. Longman 1991, Chapters 7 and 8.

On various enjoyable and thought-provoking **dictation activities**, see Davis, P and Rinvolucri, M *Dictation: new methodology, new possibilities.* Cambridge University Press 1988.

On **correcting written work**, see Byrne, D *Teaching Writing Skills* new edition. Longman 1988, Chapter 10 and Edge, J *Mistakes and Correction.* Longman 1989, Chapter 7.

Chapter 9 How to teach speaking

On **speaking activities** of various kinds, see Byrne, D *Techniques for Classroom Interaction.* Longman 1987, Nolasco, R and Arthur, L *Conversation.* Oxford University Press 1987, Ur, P *Discussions that Work.* Cambridge University Press 1981 and Harmer, J *The Practice of English Language Teaching* new edition. Longman 1991, Chapter 8.

On **correcting speaking activities**, see Edge, J *Mistakes and Correction.* Longman 1989, Chapter 6.

Chapter 10 How to teach listening

On **listening** in general, see Underwood, M *Teaching Listening Skills.* Longman 1989, Ur, P *A Course in Language Teaching.* Cambridge University Press 1996, Module 8 and Harmer, J *The Practice of English Language Teaching* new edition, Chapter 10.

On **video**, a book well worth looking at is Cooper R, Lavery, M and Rinvolucri, M *Video.* Oxford University Press 1991.

Chapter 11 How to use textbooks

The best book I know on **using textbooks** is Grant, N *Making the Most of Your Textbook.* Longman 1987. Grant's options (omit, replace, add, adapt) are paralleled by the textbook writer Richard Acklam who suggest 'SARS' (= Select, Adapt, Reject, Supplement) in a March 1994 article in *Practical English Teaching*, a magazine which is no longer published, but its publishers Mary Glasgow Magazines may be able to provide back copies.

For many ideas about **using music** in the classroom, read Cranmer, D and Laroy, C *Musical Openings.* Pilgrims Longman Resource Book. Longman 1992. For the musical activity in this chapter I used a stormy extract from the first movement of Mahler's second symphony, the last movement of Holst's St Paul's Suite, the beginning of Stravinsky's Ebony Concerto and the first movement of Tchaikovsky's String Serenade.

Chapter 12 How to plan lessons

For more on the issues surrounding **planning**, see Ur, P *A Course in Language Teaching*. Cambridge University Press 1996 Module 15, and Harmer, J *The Practice of English Language Teaching* new edition. Longman 1991, Chapter 12.

Chapter 13 What if?

On solving **classroom problems** of the kind mentioned in this chapter, a chapter called 'Dealing with constraints and problems' (Chapter 12) from Scrivener, J *Learning Teaching*. Heinemann 1994, has some very sound advice.

On the issues of **non-homogeneous classes**, a book well worth consulting is Prodromou, L *Mixed Ability Classes*. Macmillan 1992.

To get more insight into the issue of **large classes**, try reading Nolasco, R and Arthur, L *Teaching Large Classes*. Macmillan 198?.

On **disruptive students** and general issues of discipline, Wragg, E *Class Management and Control*. Macmillan 1981, is easily accessible. Underwood, M *Effective Classroom Management*. Longman 1987, Chapter 7 is clear and worth looking at. See also Harmer, J *The Practice of English Language Teaching* new edition. Longman 1991. Chapter 11.

On problems associated with **listening**, the books mentioned for Chapter 11 will have many suggestions.

Appendix A Equipment in the classroom

On the use of **boards, pictures and OHPs**, an excellent book is Wright, A and Haleem, S, *Visuals for the Language Classroom*. Longman 1991. It is also worth looking at Underwood, M *Effective Classroom Management*. Chapter 8. Longman 1987.

On the use of **dictionaries**, see Harmer, J *The Practice of English Language Teaching* new edition. Chapter 9. Longman 1991 and the instructions to the good dictionaries specially designed for students of English, of which the four most notable are the *Longman Dictionary of Contemporary English*, the *Cambridge International Dictionary of English*, the *Oxford Advanced Learners' Dictionary* and the *Collins Cobuild English Dictionary*.

On **computers**, see Hardisty, D and Windeath, S *CALL*. Oxford University Press 1989. However, the world of computers is changing so rapidly that most print material is rapidly out of date. Certainly, as far as the Internet is concerned, teachers would be advised to buy a good book on its use and start investigating for themselves.

Appendix C

Phonetic symbols

consonants	
p	**p**en, ha**pp**y, **p**ublish
b	**b**ed, ca**b**, **b**lackboard
t	**t**ime, li**tt**le, watch**ed**
d	**d**ance, play**ed**, a**d**vance
k	**c**up, **k**ind, pa**ck**
g	**g**ood, mu**g**, to**gg**le
tʃ	**ch**in, **ch**atter, ar**ch**
ʒ	plea**s**ure, vi**s**ion, deci**s**ion
dʒ	**J**uly, **g**eometry, **j**udge
f	**f**an, li**f**e, **ph**otogra**ph**
v	**v**ery, li**v**e, ad**v**ance
θ	**th**ink, pa**th**, **th**ank
ð	**th**en, mo**th**er, **th**at
s	**s**ail, **c**ell, boat**s**
z	**z**en, len**s**, lend**s**
ʃ	**sh**ell, me**sh**, **sh**ip
h	**h**e, **h**ymn, **h**and
m	**m**eet, bo**mb**, i**mm**ense
n	**n**o, ca**n**, a**n**other
ŋ	ri**ng**, si**ng**er, playi**ng**
l	**l**et, se**ll**, **l**u**ll**aby
r	**r**ing, **wr**ing, tomo**rr**ow
j	**y**es, **y**acht, opi**n**ion
w	**wh**en, **wh**at, **w**ait

vowels	
iː	sh**ee**p, br**ea**the, th**e**se
ɪ	sh**i**p, b**i**t, start**e**d
e	wh**e**n, br**ea**th, **a**ny
æ	p**a**t, b**a**ck, m**a**rry
ɑː	**ar**m, r**a**ther, h**ear**t
ɒ	cl**o**ck, wh**a**t, be**cau**se
ɔː	fl**oo**r, l**aw**, c**au**ght
ʊ	w**oo**d, w**ou**ld, w**o**man
uː	sh**oe**, sch**oo**l, J**u**ly
ʌ	**u**ncle, s**o**n, r**ou**gh
ɜː	f**ir**st, j**our**ney, **ear**th
ə	**a**gain, phot**o**graph, teach**er**
eɪ	pl**ay**, r**a**ge, gr**ea**t
əʊ	**a**go, t**ow**, th**ou**gh
aɪ	cl**i**mb, k**i**te, b**uy**
aʊ	h**ou**se, m**ou**th, cl**ow**n
ɔɪ	sp**oi**l, b**uoy**, enj**oy**
ɪə	ch**eer**, cl**ear**, w**ier**d
eə	ch**air**, wh**ere**, th**eir**
ʊə	p**ure**, l**ure**, f**ewer**

Examples:
air / eə(r) /
calm / kɑːm //
clean / kliːn /
elephant / ˈelɪfənt /
immediately / ɪˈmiːdɪətlɪ //

judgement / ˈdʒʌdʒmənt /
photography / fəˈtɒgrəfɪ /
ploy / plɔɪ /
rubbish / ˈrʌbɪʃ /
yuletide / ˈjuːltaɪd /

Index

NOTE: Index entries refer to the main body of the book (pages 1-134) and the appendices (pages 177-194) There are no index entries for the Task File.